MW01489604

TRADING FOR BEGINNERS

*Explanation on how to Master Trading bases,
Intraday and Swing Strategies, Forex, Stock
Markets, Commodities and Options through the
Correct Management of Psychology right Now*

Andrew Zone

Disclaimer

All erudition provided in this book is stated for educational and informational purpose only. The author is not in any way responsible for any outcomes or results that emerges from using this book. Constructive efforts have been made to render information that is both effective and accurate, but the author is not to be held responsible for the accuracy or use/misuse of this information.

Foreword

First, I will like to thank you for taking the first step of trusting me and deciding to purchase/read this life-transforming eBook. Thanks for spending your time and resources on this material.

I can assure you of exact results if you will diligently follow the exact blueprint, I lay bare in the information manual you are currently reading. It has transformed lives, and I strongly believe it will equally transform your own life too.

All the information I presented in this Do It Yourself piece is easy to digest and practice.

Table of Contents

INTRODUCTION

We presume you are relatively brand-new to the word "forex" and even new to trading. Possibly you have dabbled with a demonstration account, or you have some experience in other markets supplies, futures, or choices.

This book will provide you brief and vital information on things you need to know on forex trading, how one can trade successful. My goal is to provide you an extensive guide on foreign exchange.

The information in this book is meant as a brief primer of trading basics as well as mechanics.

More important to you in the long term is to chart a curriculum, personalized to meet your own specific demands and including the crucial elements of an effective trading strategy. The majority of new investors shoot from the hip when they begin.

CHAPTER ONE

Trading Bases

Firstly, let me briefly discuss the story behind trading and how it came into existence. The origins of trading dates back to primitive times, it started existing ever since men started repainting symbols on cave wall surfaces as well as understood that in exchange for a spare flint axe they might get a brand-new arrowhead head. This is exactly how all of it began. Years ago, contemporary currencies were designed; bartering was an usual way to buy and sell products, that is, to trade them straight for mutual advantage. Some 10,000 years B.C., exchanging cacao leaves for shiny blue-green rocks was as common as marketing goods as well as acquiring a new one.

Bartering, which is similar to trading, was based on two main aspects: items that were required by others and also negotiation between seller and also purchaser to get to an understanding and also seal the deal.

In time, several of the products like precious metals or barley grains came to be so very easy to trade that they were used as long-lasting media of exchange. This is just how the very first silver and gold coins emerged in various parts of the world, such as in old Greece or Persia.

Today trading cash for money is possible. In 1971, the forex market started to emerge, as international currency exchange has turned into one of the most preferred ways of trading.

Just as with the oldest forms of trading, the buying and selling of one currency for one more is done straight, without any disturbance from a third person. In addition, any person can do it online, any time as well as from anywhere.

Online trading gives you a chance be your own manager, establish your work hours, work from house (or the beach), and also permit one to make as much money as you want without the artificial cap positioned on salaries.

However, beginner investors usually have a hard time comprehending how the market functions and the information overload from trading. Enough knowledge is sufficient to keep a novice in a state of continuous trading but, they never really feel all set to take the plunge as a result of lacking the right strategies to take.

Technical advancements in the finance market have decreased the obstacles that has been stopping lot of people from trading. Currently, anyone can start generating income from the marketplaces with a basic understanding of how the marketplace functions, respectable trading capital, as well as the ideal trading tools. Actually, economic trading tools such as crawlers, trading formulas, AI, and social trading makes it simpler to become effective at trading without having actually progressed levels or any kind of specialized training.

Before getting involved in fundamentals, let's look at the different kinds of trading first:

1. Stock trading

Stock trading is the art of purchasing, holding, selling stocks (likewise called shares) of safeties listed on public stock exchanges such as NASDAQ, NYSE, and also AMEX.

2. Foreign exchange trading

Forex trading (also known as FX trading or money trading) is the art of buying and also selling money in the hopes of making revenues on the distinction in the value of such money in the worldwide economic landscape.

3. Options trading

This trading is a form of derivative trading in which individuals trade agreements that give them the civil liberties (but not obligation) to get or market an underlying asset at an established cost.

4. Binary options trading

Binary alternatives trading is a form of trading in which investors expect to gain a fixed payout or absolutely nothing in any way (they are additionally called all-or-nothing options) based on the success of their 'prediction' of the result of a specific market occasion.

CHAPTER TWO

Why You Should Trade

While most individuals begin trading to make money by becoming an effective trader, other has silver lining impacts aside from the money. And this is why I believe it's a wonderful ability to find out.

In this chapter I'm most likely to run through reasons why I think that everybody needs to find out to trade:

Trading educates you to manage your feelings

Nowadays, many trading books and sources have entire sections committed to the "trading frame of mind". That's because being able to manage your feelings is among the most crucial factors of successful trading. The idea that traders have large egos as well as are arrogant jerks is not something that holds true of contemporary successful traders. You may have been able to imitate this in the 90's when every person that bought stocks or attempted their hand at day trading, would earn money. Which is due to the fact that the stock exchange just went up and up.

The reality is that traders need to be calm and also trade without vanity. I think that trading has made me to be better at managing my emotions and this has overturned into all areas of my life including relationships.

Trading assists you deal with failure

As a result of this fact, you require to learn more about failing, as well as falling short quick. Being able to close a shedding trade as well as proceed, is something that I see newbie traders have problem with. The result is that a solitary profession can erase their entire trading account. Smart traders understand when to leave.

Having the ability to come to be comfy with short-term highs as well as short term lows will help you in all locations of life.

Trading will help you to develop a framework and also regimens

You cannot be an effective investor by logging into a trading account when a week and "looking at things," and after that having a holiday for the rest of the week. The majority of traders

I know invest a great deal of time each day checking out news, checking graphs, and so on. Lots of traders do this from residence, so without appropriate regimens, you're never most likely to succeed. So, through trading, yo can learn to get up earlier, commit time to research, etc.

Trading will make you use your money

Saving for future purpose seems wise, and we're distinguished a young age we should be doing it, however, when you do the math, that concept crumbles rather quick. If you maintain your money merely "saved" in a savings account, you're losing out to inflation.

Trading makes you use your cash. You're placing it to work. So as opposed to saving for conserving, you're now saving for investing or saving for trading. This is a lot much smarter. Now not everybody will win doing this-- traders do shed cash. But a few of you are providing yourself a shot. If you leave your cash in your checking account, in 20 years, it's going to have a great deal much less purchasing power than it does today.

Trading will certainly assist you come to be independent.

Some individuals undergo their whole lives, relying upon others without also realizing it. Trading is among the few works in the world where you can truly be independent. And even if you do not trade full-time, you're taking steps in the direction of being independent and also offering on your own a plan b in case something occurs to your full-time revenue.

CHAPTER THREE

Intraday trading

There was a time when the only people who were able to trade actively in the trading market were those benefiting big banks, brokerages, and trading houses. However, with the increase of the internet and also online trading houses, brokers have actually made it less complicated for the ordinary specific financier to get in on the video game.

Day trading can end up being a really financially rewarding career, as long as you do it correctly. But it can additionally be a little tough for newbies-- specifically for those that aren't totally prepared with a well-planned approach. Even one of the most experienced day investors can hit rough spots and also experience losses. So, what is day trading, and also how does it function?

Day investors are active traders that carry out intraday methods to make money off price adjustments for an offered asset. Day trading uses a wide variety of methods as well as methods to maximize regarded market ineffectiveness. The trading is commonly identified by technical analysis and calls for a high level of self-control and also neutrality.

The Fundamentals of Day Trading

The act of Day-trading may be explained as the purchase and also sale of a particular form of security within a single trading day. It can take place in any market but is most common in the forex (foreign exchange) and stock markets. Day traders are normally well-educated and also well-funded. They make use of high quantities of utilize and temporary trading methods to maximize small price motions in extremely liquid stocks or currencies.

Day traders are in harmony with events that cause temporary market steps. Trading information is a popular strategy. Arranged announcements such as financial data, business revenues, or rates of interest undergo market psychology and market assumptions. Markets react when those expectations are not met or are exceeded, usually with unexpected, significant moves, which can profit day traders.

These day investors use countless intraday approaches. These approaches consist of:

Scalping: Which tries to make various tiny profits on small rates modifications throughout the day.

Variety trading: This mostly uses assistance and also resistance levels to establish their deal decisions.

News-based trading: which usually confiscates trading possibilities from the heightened volatility around news occasions

High-frequency trading (HFT) techniques: That make use of advanced formulas to manipulate tiny or short-term market ineffectiveness.

The profit potential of day trading is probably among one of the most discussed and misunderstood subjects on Street. Web day trading rip-offs have actually tempted novices by promising enormous returns in a brief period. The idea that this type of trading is a get-rich-quick plan continues. Some individuals' day trade without enough knowledge. But there are day investors that make an effective living regardless of or maybe due to the risks.

Many expert money managers, as well as economic advisors, avoid day trading, saying that, in many cases, the benefit does not justify the threat. Alternatively, those that do day profession firmly insist there is revenue to be made.

Day trading profitably is feasible, yet the success price is naturally reduced because of the complexity as well as the danger of day trading in conjunction with the relevant frauds.

Additionally, economic experts and monetary professionals alike suggest that over very long periods, energetic trading approaches tend to underperform an extra standard easy index technique, specifically after costs and also tax obligations are taken into consideration.

Day trading is not for every person and also entails considerable risks. In addition, it calls for a thorough understanding of just how the markets job and also various strategies for profiting in the short-term.

While the success stories of those that struck it rich as a day trader are remembered, We also remember that most do not-- lots will certainly die and also many will barely stay afloat. Furthermore, don't undervalue the role that good luck and great timing play-- while skill is certainly a component, a rout of misfortune can sink even the most knowledgeable day investor.

Characteristics of a Day Trader

Professional day traders, those that trade for a living as opposed to as a pastime are typically reputable in the field. They typically have extensive expertise of the marketplace, too. Right here are several of the requirements required to be an effective day trader:

Expertise and experience in the marketplace

Individuals who attempt to day trade without an understanding of market fundamentals frequently lose money. Technical evaluation and also graph reading is a good ability for a day trader to have, however without an extra in-depth understanding of the marketplace you remain in and the possessions that exist because market, graphs might be tricking. Do your due diligence as well as comprehend the particular ins and outs of the items you trade.

Sufficient resources

Day investors use only equity capital which they can afford to shed. Not just does this secure them from economic wreck, however it likewise assists eliminate feeling from their trading. A large amount of funding is often essential to capitalize successfully on intraday price movements. Having accessibility to a margin account is additionally key, considering that unstable swings can sustain margin contact short notice.

Strategy

A trader needs an edge over the rest of the market. There are a number of various techniques day traders utilize consisting of swing trading, arbitrage, and trading news. These methods are refined up until they generate consistent earnings as well as efficiently restriction losses.

A rewarding approach is ineffective without discipline. Lots of day traders wind up losing a lot of cash since they fall short to make trades that satisfy their own requirements. As they state, "Plan the profession and trade the strategy." Success is impossible without technique.

To benefit, day traders rely greatly on volatility in the market. A stock may be appealing to a day trader if it moves a great deal during the day. That could occur as a result of a number of different things consisting of an earnings record, financier sentiment, or perhaps basic economic or company information.

Day investors likewise like supplies that are greatly liquid since that gives them the possibility to alter their placement without modifying the cost of the stock. If a supply price relocation higher, traders may take a buy position. If the price steps down, an investor might decide to short-sell so he can profit when it falls. Despite what technique day investors use, they normally want to trade a stock that relocates a whole lot.

Day Trading for a Living

There are two primary departments of specialist day investors: those who work alone and/or those that benefit a bigger institution. Many day traders who trade for a living help a huge organization. These investors have a benefit since they have access to a direct line, a trading work desk, huge amounts of capital, and take advantage of, pricey analytical software application, and also much more. These investors are typically looking for very easy earnings that can be made from arbitrage chances and also news events, and these sources permit them to take advantage of these much less high-risk day trades before specific traders can respond.

Specific investors frequently handle other people's money or trade with their own. Some of them have access to a trading desk, but, they usually have strong ties to a brokerage (because of the large quantities they spend on commissions) and access to various other resources. Nonetheless, the minimal scope of these sources prevents them from competing directly with institutional day investors. Instead, they are required to take more risks.

Private traders normally day trade using technical analysis as well as swing professions-- incorporated with some utilize-- to produce ample profits on such tiny cost motions in highly fluid stocks.

Day trading needs accessibility to several of one of the most intricate financial solutions and tools in the industry. Day traders generally require:

Accessibility to a trading work desk

This is normally reserved for investors benefiting bigger establishments or those who manage big amounts of money. The dealing work desk gives these investors with immediate order implementations, which are particularly crucial when sharp price activities occur. For example, when a purchase is revealed, day traders looking at merging arbitrage can place their orders before the rest of the market can take advantage of the rate differential.

Numerous information sources

News supplies the majority of possibilities where day investors take advantage of, so it is essential to be the very first to recognize when something significant occurs. The regular trading space includes accessibility to the Dow Jones Newswire, consistent protection of CNBC as well as various other news organizations, as well as software application that frequently evaluates news resources for essential tales.

Analytical software program

Trading software is a costly need for many day investors. Those that count on technical indications or swing trades depend more on software application than information.

This software application might be identified by the following:

Automatic pattern recognition: This implies the trading program recognizes technical indicators like flags and networks, or a lot of more complex signs such as Elliott Wave patterns.

Genetic as well as neural applications: These are programs that use semantic networks and hereditary formulas to ideal trading systems to make even more precise forecasts of future price movements.

Broker assimilation: Several of these applications even user interface straight with the brokerage firm which enables a rapid and even automated implementation of trades. This is practical for eliminating feeling from trading and also enhancing execution times.

Back testing: This permits traders to look at just how a particular approach would certainly have done in the past to predict much more properly how it will carry out in the future. Remember that previous efficiency is not always indicative of future outcomes.

Incorporated, these tools supply investors with a side over the remainder of the industry. It is simple to see why, without them, a lot of inexperienced investors lose money.

Should You Start Day Trading?

As stated over, day trading as a career can be hard and rather an obstacle. Initially, you require to find in with some expertise of the trading globe and have a good suggestion of your danger tolerance, capital, as well as goals.

Day trading is additionally a career that calls for a great deal of time. If you want to perfect your methods-- after you have practiced, of course-- and also generate income, you'll need to devote a lot of time to it. This isn't something you can do part-time or whenever you obtain need. You have to be completely invested in it.

If you comply with these easy guidelines, you might develop a great expertice in day trading.

All-time Low Line

Although day trading has become a debatable sensation, it can be a sensible way to make earnings. Day investors, both institutional as well as private, play an important function in the industry by maintaining the markets effective as well as fluid. While prominent among inexperienced traders, it ought to be left mainly to those with the abilities and also sources needed to be successful.

1. Knowledge Is Power

Along with expertise of fundamental trading procedures, day traders require to keep up on the current securities market news and events that impact supplies, the Fed's rates of interest plans, the economic expectation, and so on. So do your homework. Make a shopping list of supplies you 'd like to trade as well as keep on your own informed about the chosen firms and basic markets. Scan company news as well as check out dependable financial sites.

2. Reserve Funds

Evaluate just how much funding you agree to risk on each profession. Several successful day investors take the chance of less than 2% of their account per trade. If you have a $40,000 trading account as well as want to risk 0.5% of your funding on each profession, your optimum loss per profession is $200 (0.005 x $40,000). Reserve a surplus quantity of funds you can trade with as well as you are prepared to shed. Keep in mind, it might or might not happen.

3. Reserve Time Too

Day trading requires your time. That's why it's called day trading. You'll need to quit the majority of your day. Do not consider it if you have actually restricted time to spare. The procedure requires a trader to track the marketplaces as well as place opportunities, which can emerge at any moment during trading hrs. Moving quickly is key.

4. Beginning Small

As a newbie, focus on a maximum of one to two stocks during a session. Tracking and locating possibilities is simpler with just a couple of supplies.

Just recently, it has actually become increasingly common to be able to trade fractional shares, so you can define particular, smaller sized buck amounts you desire to spend. That indicates if Apple shares are trading at $250 and also you just wish to buy $50 well worth, many brokers will currently allow you buy one-fifth of a share.

5. Avoid Dime Stocks

You're probably looking for offers and also small cost, yet steer clear of from dime stocks. These supplies are frequently illiquid, as well as chances of striking a pot are frequently stark. Several stocks trading under $5 a share ended up being de-listed from relevant stock market and also are only tradable over-the-counter (OTC). Unless you see a genuine possibility as well as have done your research study, remain free from these.

6. Time Those Transactions

Numerous orders positioned by capitalists and investors begin to carry out as soon as the markets open in the early morning, which adds to price volatility. A skilled player may be able to acknowledge patterns and pick properly to make earnings. But for newbies, it may be much better to review the marketplace without making any moves for the very first 15 to 20 minutes. The middle hours are usually much less unstable, and then motion begins to grab once again toward the closing bell.

Though the rush hours provide chances, it's much safer for beginners to prevent them at first.

7. Cut Losses with Restriction Orders

Choose what type of orders you'll make use of to go into and also exit trades. Will you make use of market orders or limit orders? When you position a market order, it's executed at the very best rate offered at the time-- thus, no-cost warranty.

A limitation order, on the other hand, guarantees the cost yet, not the implementation. Limit orders help you in patronizing more precision, in which you set your cost (not unrealistic but executable) for acquiring along with selling. A lot more advanced and also skilled day investors may utilize using alternatives techniques to hedge their positions also.

8. Be Realistic Regarding Profits

A strategy doesn't require to win at all times to be rewarding. Several investors only win 50% to 60% of their professions. However, they make a lot more on their victors than they shed on their losers. Ensure the threat on each trade is limited to a certain percent of the account and that entrance, as well as departure approaches, are plainly defined as well as listed.

9. Remain Calm

There are times when the stock markets test your nerves. As a day investor, you require to discover to maintain greed, hope and also worry away. Choices must be controlled by logic as well as not emotion.

10. Stay with the Strategy

Effective investors need to scoot, but they do not need to think quickly. Why? Because they have actually created a trading method ahead of time, together with the technique to stay with that approach. It is necessary to follow your formula closely instead of attempting to chase after revenues. Don't let your feelings obtain the best of you and also abandon your method. There's a rule among day traders: "Strategy your trade and trade your plan."

Before we go into a few of the ins and outs of day trading, let's takesome of the reasons day trading can be so difficult.

What Makes Day Trading Difficult?

Day trading takes a great deal of practice and know-how, and there are several factors that can make the procedure challenging.

Firstly, know that you're taking on experts whose professions focus on trading. These individuals have accessibility to the very best technology as well as connections in the industry, so even if they stop working, they're established to prosper in the long run. If you jump on the bandwagon, it only means much more revenue for them.

People will additionally desire a cut of your profits, regardless of just how slim. Bear in mind that you'll have to pay taxes on any type of temporary gains-- or any type of investment you hold for one year or less-- at the low rate. The one caveat is that your losses are capable of offseting any gains.

As a private investor, you might be prone to psychological and also emotional prejudices. Professional investors are generally able to cut these out of their trading techniques, but when it's your very own capital involved, it often tends to be a different tale.

Determining What and also When to Acquire

Day traders try to generate income by exploiting minute cost movements in private possessions (stocks, money, futures, as well as alternatives), normally leveraging large quantities of capital to do so. In choosing what to concentrate on in a stock, claim a normal day investor seeks three points:

Liquidity: Liquidity enables you to enter as well as leave a stock at a good rate. For instance, tight spreads or the difference between the bid and ask rate of a stock, and low slippage or the distinction in between the expected rate of a profession as well as the real rate.

Volatility: Volatility is just a measure of the expected everyday price variety-- the range in which a day trader operates. Even more, volatility suggests a higher profit or loss.

Trading quantity: This is an action of the number of times supply is bought and sold in a provided period, most frequently known as the average day-to-day trading quantity. A high level of quantity shows a great deal of rate of interest in a supply. A boost in a supply's quantity is typically a precursor of a cost dive, either up or down.

How to Determine Your Entry Point?

Once you understand what type of stocks (or various other possessions) you're looking for, you need to discover just how to determine entry points, that is, at what specific minute you're going to spend. Tools that can assist you do this consist of:

1. Real-time news services: News relocates supplies, so it is essential to sign up for services that tell you when potentially market-moving information comes out.

2. ECN/Level 2 quotes: they are computer-based systems that show the very best readily available bid and ask quotes from multiple market individuals and after that instantly match and also carry out orders. Degree 2 is a subscription-based service that supplies real-time accessibility to the order composed of price quotes from market manufacturers.

Define and also jot down the problems under which you'll enter a placement. "Buy during uptrend" isn't specific enough. Something like this is much more details as well as also testable: "Get when price breaks over the top trendline of a triangle pattern, where the triangular was come before by an uptrend a minimum of one greater swing high and also higher swing low before the triangular developed on the two-minute graph in the very first two hours of the trading day.

When you have a specific collection of entry guidelines, scan via even more charts to see if those problems are produced daily, presuming you intend to day trade daily and also most of the time produce a rate move in the awaited instructions. If so, you have a prospective entrance point for an approach. You'll then require to analyze how to exit, or sell, those trades.

Determining When to Sell

There are numerous ways to leave a winning setting, consisting of routing quits and profit targets. Revenue targets are the most typical departure approach, taking a revenue at a pre-determined degree.

Target Strategy for Day Trading

1. Scalping

Scalping is one of the most prominent techniques. It entails marketing nearly quickly after a profession ends up being successful. The price target is whatever figure that translates right into "you have actually earned money on this bargain."

2. Fading

Fading entails shorting stocks after rapid moves upward. This is based on the assumption that they are overbought, early buyers prepare to start taking profits as well as existing customers might be frightened out. Although risky, this strategy can be extremely satisfying. Here, the rate target is when buyers start stepping in once more.

3. Daily Pivots

This technique involves profiting from a supply's everyday volatility. This is done by attempting to purchase the low of the day and also cost the high of the day. Here, the cost target is merely at the next indicator of a turnaround.

4. Momentum

This approach normally includes trading on news releases or locating strong trending steps sustained by high volume. One type of momentum trader will certainly purchase on press release as well as ride a trend until it shows signs of reversal. The other type will certainly fade the rate rise. Here, the price target is when volume starts to decrease.

In most cases, you'll intend to leave an asset when there is lowered rate of interest in the stock as suggested by the Degree 2/ECN and volume. The earnings target ought to also permit even more profit to be made on winning professions than is lost on losing professions. If your quit loss is $0.05 far from your entry rate, your target ought to be more than $0.05 away.

Similar to your access point, specify precisely just how you will leave your professions before entering them. The leave requirements should be specific enough to be repeatable as well as testable.

How to Restrict Losses When Day Trading

A stop-loss order is created to limit losses on a setting in security. For lengthy positions, a quit loss can be positioned listed below a current reduced, or for short settings, above a current high. It can likewise be based on volatility. For instance, if a supply price is stirring $0.05 a minute, after that you may position a quit loss

$0.15 away from your entrance to provide the price some space to fluctuate prior to it moves in your anticipated instructions.

Specify specifically just how you'll manage the threat on the professions. When it comes to a triangular pattern, as an example, a stop loss can be put $0.02 listed below a current swing reduced if purchasing an outbreak, or $0.02 listed below the pattern. (The $0.02 is arbitrary; the factor is just to be particular.).

One strategy is to establish 2 quit losses:

1. A physical stop-loss order placed at a particular price level that fits your threat tolerance. Basically, this is the most money you can stand to lose.
2. A mental stop-loss set at the point where your entry requirements are broken. This implies if the trade makes an unforeseen turn, you'll quickly exit your position.

However, you choose to leave your trades, the leave standards need to specify sufficient to be testable as well as repeatable. Also, it's important to set a maximum loss daily you can afford to withstand-- both monetarily and also emotionally. Whenever you hit this factor, take the remainder of the time off.

Adhere to your plan and also your boundaries. After all, tomorrow is an additional (trading) day.

As soon as you have actually specified just how you enter professions and also where you'll position a stop loss, you can examine whether the prospective approach fits within your threat limit. If the method exposes you to excessive danger, you require to modify the strategy in some way to decrease the risk.

If the method is within your danger limit, then testing starts. By hand experience historical charts to find your access, keeping in mind whether your quit loss or target would certainly have been struck. Paper sell in this manner for a minimum of 50 to 100 professions, noting whether the technique paid and also if it satisfies your expectations. If it does, proceed to trading the technique in a demo account in real time. If it pays over the course of 2 months or more in a simulated setting, proceed with day trading the technique with actual capital. If the approach isn't rewarding, begin again.

Ultimately, remember that if trading on margin, which means you're borrowing your investment funds from a broker agent company (and keep in mind that margin requirements for day trading are high), you're even more susceptible to sharp rate movements. Margin helps to enhance the trading results not just of profits, but of losses as well if trade breaks you. Consequently, using quit losses is critical when day trading on margin.

If you do choose that the adventure of trading is right for you, remember to start tiny. Focus on a couple of supplies instead of entering into the market head-first as well as wearing yourself thin. Going for it will complicate your trading approach and can mean big losses.

Lastly, remain cool and also try to keep the emotion out of your trades. The more you can do that, the extra you'll be able to stay with your plan. Maintaining a level head allows you to preserve your focus while maintaining you on the path you've selected to decrease.

CHAPTER FOUR

Forex In Everyday Life

The forex market (Forex, FX, or currency market) is a worldwide decentralized or non-prescription (OTC) market for the trading of money. This market helps to determine foreign exchange rates for every currency. It consists of all aspects of buying, marketing, and exchanging money at existing or figured out rates. In regards to trading volume, it is, without a doubt, the biggest market worldwide, complied with by the credit history market.

The primary participants in this market are the bigger worldwide banks. Economic centers around the globe function as supports of trading between a variety of multiple sorts of customers and vendors all the time, with the exception of weekend breaks. Given that money is always traded in pairs, the foreign exchange market does not set a currency's outright worth but instead identifies its loved one value by setting the market price of one currency if paid for with one more. Ex: US$ 1 is worth X CAD, or CHF, or JPY, and so on.

The forex market overcomes financial institutions and operates on a number of degrees. Behind the scenes, banks resort to a smaller number of financial firms referred to as "suppliers", that are involved in huge quantities of fx trading. A lot of forex suppliers are banks, so this behind the curtain market is occasionally called the "interbank market" (although a few insurers and also various other types of economic firms are included). Professions between foreign exchange suppliers can be large, involving thousands of millions of dollars. Due to the sovereignty problem when including two currencies, Forex has little (if any kind of) supervisory entity regulating its activities.

The forex market helps the global profession and also financial investments by making it possible for money conversion. As an example, it permits a business in the United States to import goods from European Union participant states, particularly Eurozone members, as well as pay Euros, despite the fact that its earnings remain in United States dollarss. It also sustains straight speculation and assessment relative to the value of currencies as well as the lug profession supposition, based upon the differential rate of interest in between two currencies.

In a normal forex transaction, a celebration purchases some amount of one money by paying with some amount of another currency.

The modern forex market started developing throughout the 1970s. This complied with three years of government constraints on fx purchases under the Bretton Woods system of monetary monitoring, which laid out the regulations for commercial and financial connections amongst the world's major commercial states after World War II. Countries slowly changed to floating currency exchange rate from the previous currency exchange rate regimen, which stayed fixed per the Bretton Woods system.

The fx market is special due to the following characteristics:

- Its significant trading volume, standing for the biggest property course on the planet causing high liquidity;
- Its geographical diffusion;
- Its continual operation: 24 hrs a day besides weekends, i.e., trading from 22:00 GMT on Sunday (Sydney) until 22:00 GMT Friday (New York);
- The range of aspects that impact exchange rates; the reduced margins of loved one profit compared to various

other markets of fixed revenue; and making use of leverage to enhance revenue and loss margins and also relative to account dimension.

Therefore, it has been referred to as the marketplace closest to the perfect of excellent competition, notwithstanding money intervention by reserve banks.

You don't necessarily need to be an investor to participate in the forex market. Every single time you take a trip and also need to trade some cash right into an international money, you are joining it.

Think of that you have actually just gotten here in New York from Paris. You intend to purchase a burger at the airport terminal, however you only have euros on you. So you'll need some US dollars if you do not intend to see New York on an empty tummy.

So you go to the very first forex desk at the airport, as well as exchange your euros into United States dollars. Whether you think it or otherwise, this is the very first step of what we call forex trading.

Wait a min! You traded 10 euros as well as came back 12. 74 US bucks. Just how's that possible? This is the real exchange rate that made you richer.

After a couple of days, you wave goodbye to the Statue of Liberty and take a flight to Berlin. You trade your remaining US bucks right into euros. Hey, what occurred? You got back less than you anticipated ... Why? While you were in New York City, the currency exchange rate transformed. Why? That's due to inflation, financial modifications, and the balance between supply and also need, to only call a few of the factors that can affect the worth of a currency.

What is foreign exchange trading?

Forex, or foreign exchange, can be explained as a network of customers and sellers, that move money between each other at a concurred rate. It is the methods by which individuals, business and also reserve banks convert one currency right into an additional-- if you have actually ever before travelled abroad, then it is likely you have actually made a foreign exchange deal.

While a great deal of foreign exchange is done for useful objectives, the vast bulk of money conversion is carried out with the purpose of earning some earnings. The amount of money transformed on a daily basis can make price movements of some money exceptionally unstable. It is this volatility that can make foreign exchange so appealing to traders: producing a greater possibility of high revenues, while additionally raising the danger.

Discover a series of other advantages of foreign exchange trading.

Unlike shares or assets, foreign exchange trading does not take place on exchanges but straight between 2 celebrations, in an over the counter (OTC) market. The forex market is run by a global network of financial institutions, spread out across four significant forex trading centers in different time zones: London, New York, Sydney and also Tokyo. Because there is no main location, you can trade forex 24 hours a day.

There are three different sorts of forex market:

Spot foreign exchange market: the physical exchange of a money pair, which occurs at the exact factor the trade is cleared up e.g. on the spot' or within a short amount of time.

Onward foreign exchange market: a contract is consented to buy or market a set quantity of a currency at a defined price, to be worked out at a set date in the future or within a series of future dates.

Future foreign exchange market: a contract is accepted purchase or offer a set quantity of a provided money at a set cost as well as date in the future. Unlike forwards, a futures agreement is legally binding.

Many investors hypothesizing on foreign exchange rates will not intend to take distribution of the currency itself; rather they make currency exchange rate forecasts to make the most of rate motions on the market.

What is a base and also quote money?

A base currency is the initial currency provided in a foreign exchange set, while the second currency is called the quote currency. Foreign exchange trading always entails marketing one currency in order to acquire another, which is why it is priced estimate in pairs-- the rate of a forex pair is just how much one device of the base money is worth in the quote currency.

Each currency in the pair is listed as a three-letter code, which often tends to be created of two letters that stand for the region, and also one representing the currency itself. As an example, GBP/USD is a money pair that involves getting the Great British extra pound as well as offering the US buck.

So in the example listed below, GBP is the base money while USD is the quote money. If GBP/USD pair is trading at 1.35361, then one pound deserves about 1.35361 dollars.

If the pound rises against the dollar, then a single pound will certainly deserve more bucks and the pair's rate will enhance. If it goes down, the pair's price will certainly lower. So if you believe that the base currency in a set is likely to strengthen against the quote money, you can acquire the pair (going long). If you believe it will weaken, you can market the pair (going short).

To maintain points ordered, many service providers divided sets right into the following classifications:

Major pairs. Seven currencies that compose 80% of global forex trading. Includes EUR/USD, USD/JPY, GBP/USD, USD/CHF, USD/CAD as well as AUD/USD.

Minor sets. Less frequently traded, these commonly feature major currencies against each other instead of the United States dollar. Includes: EUR/GBP, EUR/CHF, GBP/JPY.

Example of major currency matched with a currency from an emerging or small economy includes: GBP/MXN (Sterling vs Mexican peso), USD/PLN (US dollar vs Polish zloty), EUR/CZK.

Regional pairs. Pairs classified by area-- such as Scandinavia or Australasia. Consists of: EUR/NOK (Euro vs Norwegian krona), AUD/NZD (Australian buck vs New Zealand buck), AUD/SGD.

What moves the forex market?

The foreign exchange market is comprised of money from all over the world, which can make currency exchange rate predictions hard as there are several factors that might add to price movements. However, like most economic markets, foreign exchange is largely driven by the pressures of supply and also needs, and also it is important to gain an understanding of the influences that drives rate fluctuations below.

Reserve banks.

Reserve banks manage supply, that can introduce procedures that will have a considerable impact on their currency's cost. Quantitative reducing, for instance, entails injecting even more money right into an economic climate, and also can cause its currency's price to drop.

Report.

Business banks and also other financiers tend to intend to place their resources into economic situations that have a strong expectation. So, if a positive item of information strikes the marketplaces concerning a certain area, it will motivate investment and rise need for that region's money.

Unless there is an identical rise in supply for the currency, the variation in between supply and need will certainly cause its cost to boost. Similarly, a piece of unfavorable information can create financial investment to decrease as well as reduce a currency's rate. This is why currencies often tend to mirror the reported financial health of the region they represent.

Market sentiment.

Market sentiment, which frequents reaction to the news, can also play a major function in driving currency costs. If traders think that a currency is headed in a particular instruction, they will trade appropriately as well as might persuade others to follow suit, increasing or decreasing demand.

Economic data.

Economic data is integral to the price movements of currencies for two reasons-- it gives an indication of how an economy is performing, and it offers insight into what its central bank might do next.

Say, for example, that inflation in the Eurozone has risen above the 2% level that the European Central Bank (ECB) aims to maintain. The ECB's main policy tool to combat rising inflation is increasing European interest rates-- so traders might start buying the euro in anticipation of rates going up. With more traders wanting euros, EUR/USD could see a rise in price.

Credit rating rankings

Capitalists will certainly try to maximize the return they can receive from a market, while minimizing their threat. So along with rates of interest as well as economic information, they might additionally look at credit score rankings when determining where to invest.

A country's credit history rating is an independent analysis of its likelihood of settling its debts. A nation with a high debt rating is seen as a safer location for investment than one with a low credit history score. This usually enters into particular emphasis when credit rating ratings are upgraded and devalued. A nation with an upgraded credit history ranking can see its money rise in price, and also the other way around.

CHAPTER FIVE

How Foreign Exchange Trading Works

There are a variety of different manner in which you can trade foreign exchange, yet they all work the same way: by simultaneously buying one currency while offering one more. Traditionally, a great deal of forex deals has actually been made by means of a forex broker, however with the surge of on the internet trading you can benefit from forex price movements making use of by-products like CFD trading.

CFDs are leveraged items, which allow you to open up a setting for a just a portion of the full value of the profession. Unlike non-leveraged products, you don't take possession of the property, yet take a setting on whether you think the marketplace will increase or fall in value. Although leveraged products can magnify your profits, they can also magnify losses if the market moves versus you.

What is the spread in foreign exchange trading?

The spread is the distinction in between the deal prices quoted for a forex pair. Like lots of monetary markets, when you open a foreign exchange setting you'll be presented with two rates. If you want to open up a long position, you trade at the buy price, which is slightly above the market price. If you wish to open up a short setting, you trade at the sell rate-- slightly below the marketplace rate.

What is a whole lot in forex?

Money are traded in whole lots, sets of currency made use of to standardize foreign exchange trades. As forex has a tendency to relocate percentages, whole lots have a tendency to be large: a common lot is 100,000 units of the base currency. So, due to the fact that private traders won't necessarily have 100,000 extra pounds (or whichever money they're trading) to position on every profession, almost all forex trading is leveraged.

Advantage of forex

Leverage is the ways of gaining exposure to large amounts of currency without needing to pay the amount of your profession upfront. Rather, you take down a tiny down payment, known as margin. When you close a leveraged position, your profit or loss is based upon the full dimension of the trade.

While that does amplify your profits, it also brings the danger of enhanced losses, including losses that can exceed your margin. Leveraged trading as a result makes it incredibly important to find out how to handle your threat

Margin of forex

Margin is a crucial part of leveraged trading. It is the term utilized to explain the initial down payment you put up to open and maintain a leveraged placement. When you are trading foreign exchange with margin, keep in mind that your margin demand will transform depending upon your broker, and also how large your profession dimension is.

Margin is generally expressed as a portion of the full position. So, a profession on EUR/GBP, for example, might only require 1% of the complete worth of the placement to be paid in order for it to be opened. So rather than transferring AUD$ 100,000, you 'd just need to deposit AUD$ 1000.

What is a pip in forex?

Pips are the units utilized to determine activity in a foreign exchange pair. A forex pip is typically comparable to a one-digit motion in the 4th decimal place of a currency pair. So, if GBP/USD steps from \$1.35361 to \$1.35371, after that it has moved a solitary pip. The decimal places revealed after the pip are called fractional pips, or often pipettes.

The Forex market is just one of one of the most diverse, busy markets around. Banks, businesses, federal governments, financiers and also traders involve trade as well as guess on money in the Forex market which also is referred to as the 'Fx market', 'Foreign money market', 'Foreign exchange money market' or 'Currency market'.

It is the biggest and also most fluid market worldwide. The day-to-day traded volume changes frequently, but according to the Bank for International Settlements (BIS), trading in the foreign exchange market balanced \$5.1 trillion in April 2016.

The numerous trading sessions of the forex market can be separated into 3 significant groups;

The very first being the Asian session which covers the Wellington, Sydney as well as Tokyo sessions. This continues into the begin of the second session which is

The European/London session. This is the biggest session in terms of volume, transactions and volatility, making up over 37% of all forex trading activity throughout the globe.

The last session is the NY/US session which starts around 8am EST as well as proceeds till 5pm EST. This is the second biggest session by quantity as well as transactions.

How You Can Trade In The Forex Market

The fx market permits you to deal a currency of any kind of nation versus an additional money.

To offer you the most fundamental instance of just how you can trade the forex market as well as profit, if you believe the Euro is going to rise vs. the USD, then you would certainly buy it vs. the USD using the EUR/USD set. On the other hand, if you assume the Euro is most likely to fall in worth, after that you would certainly offer it vs. the USD. This is the standard technician of foreign exchange trading.

Basic Features of The Forex Market

There is no central trading exchange in the fx market vs the stock exchange (e.g. New York Stock Exchange). All forex professions are carried out electronically, non-prescription (OTC) with the prices quoted by the significant banks. There are about 13 significant banks which do this, hence, not all financial institutions will have the exact same exact rate on money.

Extremely Liquid + 24 Hour Trading

The fx market is very liquid (over $5 trillion a day) which makes certain that a capitalist can deal a currency at basically any type of point of time with lower trading prices than for instance stocks. It also implies you can get a much better rate than trading stocks due to the fact that there are much more purchasers as well as vendors, therefore even more pricing offered.

Additionally, unlike stocks, a retail foreign exchange investor can make money (as well as to be reasonable, shed!) in both rising and falling markets. With stocks, it is much more challenging to go 'short' (trying to benefit from a fall in cost in supplies), hence you have a lot more competitive advantages in trading the foreign exchange market. This makes it much easier to profit in bull and also bearishness vs trading supplies.

Daily fluctuations in the money are often much less unstable than stocks, many times less than 1% adjustment in the worth of the money. This is why several forex traders depend on the take advantage of to boost the worth of possible movements. In the retail foreign exchange trading world, take advantage of can be as high as 250:1 (although we advise no greater than 100:1 for Non-EU). With 100:1 take advantage of, you can trade $100 well worth of a particular money with only $1, providing you a chance to benefit from the average daily activities in the fx markets and currency pairs.

Forex Brokers

Forex brokers play a vital role in the fx market as they are the essential link between the individual (you the retail Forex investor) as well as the forex market. Specific capitalists cannot trade the foreign exchange market straight via the major financial institutions (unless you have at the very least $1 million USD).

Brokers profit by supplying private financiers and also investors (like you) a chance to trade the fx market simply through matching purchasers and also vendors.

It's important to comprehend the foreign exchange market is not an absolutely no sum video game (indicating one purchaser for each and every vendor). Many times smaller traders (retail investors) make professions that are matched by one large buyer/seller, and both of you can make money. This occurs with larger fx players having different holding times or rates than you.

So an instance is you acquire the Euro vs. the USD at 1.15 as well as have a target of 1.16. At the same time the larger gamer has a target at 1.10. If the price rises to 1.16, you make money, while the larger gamer can hold the setting for a bigger move, maybe later to 1.10. The key to recognize in all of this is that the forex market is not an absolutely no amount game, and both purchasers and sellers can benefit. Understand, nevertheless, that they can additionally shed.

How Forex Brokers Make Money

The key method foreign exchange brokers make money is by the spread, which is the distinction between the Bid and also Ask price for a currency set. Consider it like exactly how a property broker finds a customer (you) for a residence that is being sold (by the vendor). The spread is a little markup in rate from the actual currency pair.

The second method a forex broker usually earnings is from billing commissions. This is usually certain to the sort of account you have, and also just how much trading volume you do each month. Most of fx brokers today do not bill compensations, but see to it to get in touch with any potential broker you register with.

Why has the foreign exchange market come to be so preferred?

Learning exactly how to trade and make consistent revenues is not an easy thing. However, if you can learn just how to trade foreign exchange successfully, it can use a lifestyle that cannot be contrasted to most other tasks. This is because you can function from house, or profession from anywhere in the globe as long as you have an internet link and a laptop.

Imagine having the ability to function from anywhere in the globe, wearing whatever clothing you wish to, operating at whatever time you want to, while vacationing, taking a trip, home or at the coffeehouse. These are several of the many factors trading foreign exchange has drawn in numerous traders to the fx market over the last years. If you agree to work hard and also learn the necessary abilities for forex trading, you can end up being a full- or part-time fx investor.

I personally was tired of working in a workplace, having others inform me what to do, what to put on, when I made money, when I obtained a raising, and also just how much I'm worth. If you intend to work from house and also have no restriction to how much money you can make (understanding that there is constantly run the risk of involved when you trade!), then you ought to definitely find out exactly how to trade the forex markets. Along those lines, below are a few of the core abilities which are essential to you ending up being an effective and also successful forex investor. These skills can be learned and also strengthened through way of thinking publications and/or frame of mind training courses.

Tips To Be A Successful Trader

Discipline: Good self-control is very vital for any foreign exchange trader. Having excellent technique guarantees you are able follow your trading strategy (policies) consistently, while preventing inadequate trading opportunities.

Effective fx trading is everything about rigorous threat and money management which is difficult if you do not have the technique needed to continually adhere to your guidelines. Think of it how a professional casino poker gamer finds out to make money from rewarding hands, fold weak ones and protect their bankroll.

Investors having a hard time to make consistent earnings trading the fx markets often show poor discipline, continually violating their trading strategy and also threat- and also finance guidelines. Nobody comes to be a professional football player by having inadequate self-control.

Strength: New investors oftentimes are very ecstatic and determined to discover how to trade foreign exchange successfully, specifically with the chance to work from home and generate income throughout the globe, 24 hours a day.

Understanding just how to trade requires time, much like it takes numerous months and even years to come to be skilled in speaking a new language. It will certainly likewise test your state of mind and technique, similar to it takes a lot more effort to enter physical form than you anticipate.

The process of finding out to trade effectively will call for strength, or the capability to endure ups and also downs (similar to any kind of occupation or service). Therefore, have the assumption from the outset you will likely have to function more difficult than you expect.

What are the Advantages of Trading the Forex Market?

As discussed in the past, the foreign exchange market can be traded anywhere in the globe as all trading is done online. Thus you can trade forex from throughout the globe as long as you have a laptop as well as a net link.

The high liquidity of the Forex market implies you can go into or exit a trade/position immediately, contrasted to specific stocks where (in the most awful in4stance) can be 'stuck' in a position due to the fact that there is no buyer or vendor readily available.

You can profit (as well as obviously lose!) in both fluctuating markets trading forex, unlike supplies, which you typically can just acquire as a retail investor.

Rather than working your method through the jungle of thousands of supplies, you can focus on a few money pairs only, using numerous high likelihood trading possibilities 24 hrs. a day because of the constant volatility and liquidity in the foreign exchange market.

If you are most likely to discover exactly how to trade foreign exchange with, you'll need to pick up from a forex training course or by dealing with a tried and tested forex advisor and forex trader. Only after that can you know if your trading mentor's strategies and methods work. One excellent way to figure out the top quality of a forex advisor and/or foreign exchange training program is to see how well the students are doing by checking out foreign exchange success stories.

You may listen to how you require to find out technical analysis or find out about basic trading to earn money trading forex. It's essential to understand, that while financial institutions, hedge funds, prop firms, as well as specific traders might use these approaches to place trades in the market, all those choices are based upon one variable-- information.

No matter exactly how they obtain the information, that 'details' needs to be become an 'order' or a profession (i.e. I wish to purchase the EUR/USD at 1.1500). All of these 'orders' integrated are what is called 'order circulation.

Because we do not have direct accessibility to the order flow in the foreign exchange market, we need to discover exactly how to review its 'impact', which is consisted of in the cost action which is visible on all forex trading period. Rate activity has the fingerprints of order flow throughout it. This is why you have to find out rate action trading.

When research found out can be done on any instrument, forex set, trading period or setting (up/down fad, ranging market, high or reduced volatility).

The skill of having the ability to review foreign exchange cost's motion in time will certainly allow you to see where the institutional players are more involved (purchasing or marketing).

- where are key assistance and resistance areas?
- where to find precise entry and also leaves (trade areas).
- whether the marketplace will breakout to new highs or lows.
- how to generate income in foreign exchange pattern trading.
- locating tops and also bases in trends.
- what are impulsive vs. rehabilitative price action relocations.
- what kind of market setting you remain in (bull/bear pattern, array, low/high volatility).

CHAPTER SIX

What Time Frame Should I Trade

One of the factors newbie foreign exchange investors don't do along with, is because they're normally trading the wrong timespan for their individuality.

New forex traders will certainly intend to get rich quick so they'll begin trading small time structures like the 1-minute or 5-minute graphs.

After that they wind up obtaining irritated result when they trade since the moment framework does not fit their individuality, know which timespan you must trade on as a foreign exchange trader. For some forex investors, they really feel most comfortable trading the 1-hour graphs.

This time around framework is longer, however not too long, and trade signals are less, yet not as well few. Trading on this time around structure helps give even more time to evaluate the marketplace and not feel so hurried.

On the other hand, we have a good friend that might never ever sell a 1-hour period. It would be way as well sluggish for him, and also he 'd probably believe he was going to rot and also pass away before he can enter a profession. He chooses to trade a 10-minute chart. It still provides him adequate time (but not way too much) to make decisions based upon his trading plan. An additional buddy of ours can't find out exactly how foreign exchange investors trade on a 1-hour chart because he thinks it's also quick! He trades just daily, weekly, and also regular monthly graphs. Okay, so you're probably asking what the correct time frame is for you. Well friend, if you had been listening, it relies on your personality. You need to feel comfortable with the time framework you're trading in. You'll constantly really feel some kind of stress or feeling of stress when you're in a trade since actual cash is included.

Yet you shouldn't feel that the reason for the pressure is because points are occurring so quickly that you locate it challenging to choose or two gradually that you get discouraged. When we first started trading, we couldn't stick to a time frame. We started with the 15-minute graph, after that the 5-minute graph. After that we attempted the 1-hour graph, the everyday chart, and also the 4-hour chart.

This is natural for all new forex investors up until you locate your convenience area as well as why we suggest that you DEMO profession utilizing various time frames to see which fits your individuality the best.

CHAPTER SEVEN

Introduction To Forex Charting

This chapter of the book will give you a brief summary of the three primary kinds of graphs that you will run across in your Forex trading trip. I feel forex candlestick charts do the most effective work at showing the cost dynamics in a market, since their design helps you to envision the "force", or absence thereof, that a specific rate activity showed. So, let's look at the 3 major kinds of graphs that you will likely view as you trade the marketplaces:

1. **Line graphs**

Line charts are proficient at offering you a fast sight of overall market fad along with support as well as resistance degrees. They are not actually functional to compromise of because you can't see the private rate bars, however if you wish to see the fad of the marketplace in a clear way, you should take a look at the line graphs of your preferred markets periodically.

Line charts are made by attaching a line from the high rate of one period to the high price of the following, reduced to low, open up to open, or near shut.

Without a doubt, line charts that show a connection from one closing cost to the next are one of the most helpful as well as the most commonly utilized; this is because the closing rate of a market is deemed one of the most crucial, since it determines who won the battle in between the bulls as well as the bears for that time period.

Let's check out an example of a day-to-day line chart of the EURUSD

2. Bar charts

A bar chart reveals to us a cost bar for each and every period of time. So, if you are looking at a daily graph you will see a price bar for every day, a 4-hour graph will reveal you one cost bar for every 4-hour amount of time and so on. A specific price bar provides us 4 items of info that we can use to help us make our trading decisions: The open, high, reduced, and close, you will certainly sometimes see bar charts called OHLC charts (open, high, reduced, close charts), bellow's an example of one price bar.

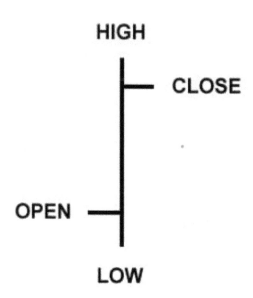

Below's an example of the very same EURUSD chart we made use of for the line graph example but as a bar chart:

3. Candle Stick Charts

Candle stick Charts reveal the same details as a bar chart yet in a visual layout that is extra fun to consider. Candle stick charts suggest the low and high of the given period equally as bar charts do, with an upright line. The top upright line is called the top shadow while the bottom vertical line is called the reduced darkness; you might likewise see the top and also lower darkness described as "wicks". The primary difference lies in just how candlestick charts show the opening and also closing rate. The large block in the middle of the candlestick suggests the variety between the opening and also closing cost. Commonly this block is called the "genuine body".

Typically, if the actual body is filled in, or darker in color the money shut less than it opened up, and also if the actual body is left unfilled, or usually a lighter shade, the currency shut higher than it opened. For example, if the actual body is white or one more light color, the top of the real body most likely indicates the close cost and all-time low of the real body shows the open price. If the real body is black or another dark color, the top of the real body likely shows the open cost and also all-time low shows the close rate (I made use of words "most likely" considering that you can make the actual body whatever shade you want). This will all become clear with an illustration:

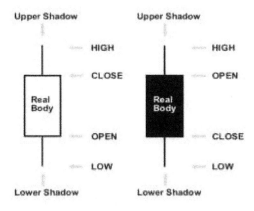

Now, below is the same EURUSD day-to-day graph that I showed you in line and also bar form, as a candle holder chart. Note that I have made the candle lights black and white, you can pick whatever shades you want, just make certain they get along to your eye but also that they communicate favorable as well as bearishness to you. Favorable candle lights are the white ones (close higher than open) and also bearish candles are the black ones (close less than open):

Candlestick graphs are the most preferred of all three significant graph types, and also because of this, they are the kind you will certainly see usually as you trade, as well as they are also the type I suggest you utilize when you find out and also patronize price activity strategies. I make use of candle holder charts in my Forex trading course, and also I suggested all my participants use them when posting up charts in the members' online forum, since their visual pleasantness as well as simplexes make it much easier for everybody to gain from.

CHAPTER EIGHT

Trading Strategies

There are many different Forex trading approaches. Nevertheless, there are some fundamentals of checking out a rate graph that you need to understand before you can go on to learning any kind of extensive strategy. Let's cover the basic building blocks of trading the Forex market from a technological analysis approach:

Support and Resistance degrees

Support degrees are produced as a market turns higher. So, if a market is moving lower as an example and it after that changes instructions and also starts relocating higher, it either has actually created a level of assistance or bounced off a formerly existing degree of assistance.

Resistance levels are produced as a market turns reduced. So, if a market is moving higher as an example, and it after that changed instructions and also beings moving reduced, it either has created a degree of resistance or jumped off a previously existing degree of resistance:

Recognizing and also plotting support and also resistance levels is by no means an exact science. Instead, it calls for making use of the discerning human eye as well as a bit of mind power do not be worried though, it's actually not that challenging to become skilled and also certain in attracting assistance as well as resistance degrees on your graphs.

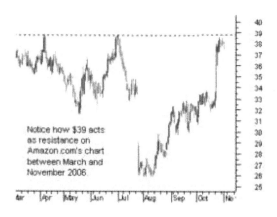

Notice how $39 acts
as resistance on
Amazon.com's chart
between March and
November 2006

Now, one important factor that I desire you to learn about assistance and also resistance levels is that they are not concrete. Numerous investors seem to assume assistance and resistance degrees are concrete which they need to never trade a setup if there is a support or resistance level close by, this can lead to them obtaining evaluation paralysis as well as never ever entering a profession. While it is true that you require to think about the key assistance and also resistance degrees in the market, you also require to check out the general market problem. You see, in trending markets, support and resistance degrees will typically be damaged by the fad momentum; so do not hesitate of support and also resistance levels, as they will typically damage. Instead, watch these levels for trading signals.

You see, when a Forex trading signal like a cost action configuration is at a crucial support or resistance degree, it is a really high-probability even to take notice of.

Trend trading

Trending markets provide us the best chance to receive earnings, considering that the market is moving in one general direction; we can use this info to our benefit by looking to go into the market towards the pattern.

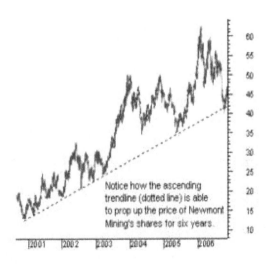

Notice how the ascending trendline (dotted line) is able to prop up the price of Newmont Mining's shares for six years.

An uptrend is marked by a collection of higher highs and also greater lows, as well as a sag is noted by a collection of lower highs and reduced lows. Keep in mind that patterns do finish, as we can see in the everyday EURUSD graph, the drop has pertained to an end lately after the pattern of reduced highs and reduced lows was broken.

I like to trade with the near-term everyday fad by seeking high-probability rate activity techniques forming within the structure of the market trend.

What I suggest by this is basically looking for cost action configurations developing near support as a market turns lower in an uptrend and near resistance as a market revolves greater in a sag. Markets ups and downs, and if you can learn to capitalize on trending markets, you will certainly have an excellent shot at becoming a successful Forex trader:

Counter-trend trading

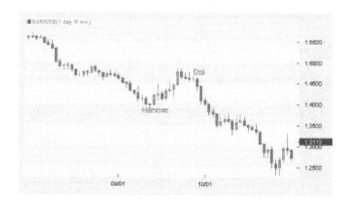

Since trends do end, we can additionally make use of this info. However, counter-trend trading is naturally riskier and also harder than trading with the fad, so it needs to just be tried after you have totally understood trading with the pattern. Some of the important things to seek in a good counter-trend signal is a price activity pattern or configuration developing at a very evident and also 'key' assistance or resistance level on the daily graph.

Range-bound market trading

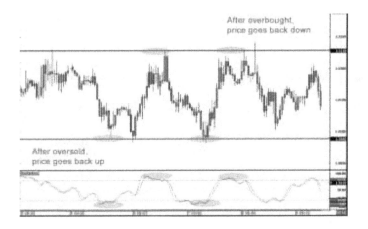

When a market is in a trading variety it implies that it is settling between a level of assistance as well as resistance. We can make use of the fact that a market is jumping between support as well as resistance to our benefit. As the market approaches the assistance or resistance limit of the trading array, we have a high-probability entry level, since threat is plainly defined just over or listed below the resistance or assistance of the array. When trading cost activity in trading arrays, you can look for apparent rate activity configurations creating near the borders of the variety, see right here:

Forex Candle stick charts and patterns

Forex graphs however as they are extremely crucial to the manner in which I trade and also educate price activity, I intended to provide a bit even more time. It's important to understand that candle holder patterns have particular terminology all to their self that you ought to come to be acquainted with before you attempt to grasp a trading method like price activity.

While we are discussing different methods of trading the Forex market, I wish to discuss what I really feel is an extensively believed "myth" relating to automated robot as well as indicator-based trading systems.

You are possibly going to come across lots of Forex web site selling Forex software that they assert will fully mechanize the process of trading, to make sure that all you have to do is click your mouse when the software tells you to and then rake in the earnings. You require to frequently keep in mind the old stating "If it appears as well great to be real it possibly is" when you are learning to trade Forex.

Like I claimed previously, you are most likely to find a great deal of these robotic web sites if you have not already. You are best served by neglecting them all together.

You will most likely see performance history that they claim are "undeniable" evidence of the robotics efficiency in the marketplace, what they don't inform you is that this track record is merely a display of a "perfect" collection of data that the software was back-tested on. The point is that trading software cannot work over the lasting since the market is continuously altering and also thus, it takes the discerning discretion of the human brain to trade the marketplaces over the lasting successfully.

I am not claiming that computer system software has no area in trading, but it cannot be the only thing you depend on, as well as it certainly must not be used in an attempt to fully automate the trading process. The ability to read the raw cost action of a market and grow and develop with the ever-changing problems of the market is just how I personally profession as well as just how I instruct my pupils to trade.

CHAPTER NINE

Swing Strategy

If you were to take a swing trading training course now, I think that the current market problems would certainly permit any investor making use of the correct trading strategy to accomplish strong results. There are a few points that I believe we should consider before getting started.

One of those is to establish if we ought to trade a countertrend system or a trending stock arrangement. Either one can work, yet it depends on you to identify which one you wish to use. I suggest utilizing paper trading on a supply turn the next time you see one create.

This chapter is most likely to go extensive concerning a vital swing trading technique on daily charts. While this might be taken into consideration innovative swing trading, this approach is suitable for all investors. It is excellent for residence research. We will tell you just how to do appropriate technological analysis and also show you when to go into the profession and when to exit the trade. We will certainly do this by mentor you how to set the right earnings target.

It is necessary to see to it you have a totally established training strategy prior to starting to trade any type of swing trading system. This will aid you prepare to end up being much more successful and sign up with the ranks of expert day investors. It is our goal to give you the trading possibilities, along with assistance you in every manner in which we can to become the very best swing investors around. You can also learn the means lenders sell the foreign exchange market.

What is Swing Trading?

Swing trading strategies are quite straightforward. Utilizing an intermediate timeframe (usually a few days to a few weeks), swing traders will recognize market patterns as well as employment opportunities. The name swing trading originates from the fact that we are trying to find conditions where rates are most likely to turn either upwards or downwards.

Swing traders can use a wide range of technological signs. What makes swing trading special is that it mixes several parts of day trading, with the rate of position trading. Swing trading signs are mainly used to discover patterns that play out between 3 and also 15 trading durations. After we evaluate these durations, we will be able to determine whether instances of resistance or assistance have happened.

The next action is to determine the bearish or bullish trend and also look for turnarounds. Reversals are typically described as pullbacks or countertrends. Once the countertrend becomes clear, we can choose our access point.

The goal is to become part of a placement where the countertrend will rapidly turn around and costs will certainly swing. This is specifically what allowed Jesse Livermore to earn most of his ton of money.

Before diving into some of the essential policies that make a swing trading strategy work, let's very first analyze the benefits of using an easy swing trading technique.

What Are the Advantages of a Simple Swing Trading Strategy?

The primary advantage of swing trading is that it supplies terrific risk to reward trading chances. In other words, you're most likely to take the chance of a smaller quantity of your account balance for potentially much larger earnings, compared to your risk.

The 2nd benefit of using swing trading approaches that work is that they get rid of a lot of the intraday sound. Currently you'll be trading like the smart money does, which is in the large swing waves.

The 3rd advantage of swing trading relies on making use of technological indicators. Utilizing technical indications can decrease the dangers of speculative trading as well as assist you to explain choices. While some swing traders pay attention to basic indicators also, they are not needed for our easy strategies.

The last benefit of using a basic swing trading strategy is that you won't require to be glued to the screen for the entire day like with day trading strategies. A swing trading plan will operate in all markets beginning with stocks, commodities, Forex money and a lot more.

Like any kind of trading method, turn trading also has a couple of threats. Because swing trading techniques take a number of days or perhaps weeks to play out, you encounter the threats of "voids" in trading over night or over the weekend.

Another risk of swing trading is that abrupt turnarounds can develop shedding placements. Due to the fact that you are not trading all throughout the day, it can be easy to be caught off guard if price trends do not play out as planned. To reduce the risk of this happening, we suggest providing stop orders with every new placement. Stop orders can assist you "lock-in" your gains and can likewise assist you reduce your losses.

There are numerous various trading strategies that you may select to adopt as a Forex trader, as well as in the adhering to guide we will be looking at something known as Swing Trading.

Swing Trading is a method of aiming to secure revenues over several days, instead of having a short term view of securing earnings as you would certainly be utilizing if as an example you chose to place extremely short-term professions such as 60 second trades.

The ways in which an investor will utilize a Swing Trading approach is to maximize their gains, over several days however by reducing their threat by locations a lot smaller valued professions on their currencies pairings, as well as slowly however undoubtedly take advancement of even the tiniest activities in currency worth.

Nevertheless, it must be kept in mind that is the timing of trades put when making use of a swing trading technique that is one of the most important facet of this method of trading, as you do need to time your trades to ideal by utilizing a series of different tools.

In the adhering to guide we will consider ways you can start to take into place your own special sort of swing trading technique, as well as whilst it might take you some time to excellent this way of trading, it can be a really lucrative means, over the long-term, to secure ongoing revenues on the money markets.

1. Swing Trading Budget

One fascinating facet of using a Swing Trading technique is that are you are just wanting to make small minimum valued profit on a collection of professions positioned over a number of days, you are not always most likely to require a huge trading spending plan to adopt this type of method.

You will as a result locate that as a very first time investor or one which does not wish to have to risk large quantities of cash positioning currency pairings this may be an approach that will attract you.

Whereas an investor utilizing for example a Day Trading method is wanting to make revenues of around 5 to 10 percent of their general trading spending plan, you are going to be aiming to make much smaller gains on each profession you put.

So you can as well as will just require to aim to make trading revenue of one or two percent of your general trading spending plan when Swing Trading.

2. Selecting the Currency Pairings

Of course, you will certainly have great deals of different currencies parings that you can pair with each other when using any kind of trading approach and also this holds true with a swing trading approach too.

Before you put your trades, you ought to designate a day or a variety of hours whereby you are proactively looking for information that is most likely to enable you to make a good and also well thought out choice on the currencies you will certainly be pairing together.

So, make sure you are totally upgraded with monetary information as well as information tales and day that is due to be launched during the week which is most likely to have an instant effect on the value of any significant money.

If you think that any one country is most likely to have some poor economic data formally announced then that will certainly be one of the most likely countries money that you will be looking to have on one side of your sell the following week and pair it up with a nations money that is most likely to stay strong or perhaps obtain in value in the coming days.

3. Making Use Of Trader Bonuses

A first time or inexperienced forex trader is often going to be overwhelmed by the sheer variety of foreign exchange trader incentives they can use when they register to a forex broker and also make a preliminary deposit into their freshly opened actual cash trading account.

Nonetheless, whilst such bonus offers are obviously going to give you a much bigger trading budget plan, you need to keep in mind that you are most likely to be required to have to place a specific volume of Forex patronizes the perk funds prior to the materialize money funds.

As you are most likely to be placing lots of trades over several days as a swing trader then rewards might serve in assisting you protect a profit on your professions. Nevertheless, watch for those on which you are only required to put a little volume of professions to turn your reward funds right into genuine money funds, as they supply the best value for all Forex traders.

Swing Trading Indicators You Need to Know:

Bollinger Bands Indicator: This is a technical indication created by John Bollinger. Bollinger Bands are developed to find overbought as well as oversold area out there. They also determine the marketplace volatility.

The swing trading indicator makes it very easy to manage the dangers of trading and additionally take advantage of price changes. Making use of a candlestick trading chart can likewise be handy. These graphs provide even more info than an easy price graph and likewise make it easier to figure out if a sustained turnaround will happen.

Numerous swing investors additionally maintain a close watch out for multi-day chart patterns.

- Head Shoulders Patterns
- Flag Patterns
- Cup and Handle Patterns
- Moving Average Crossovers (additionally take into consideration the Ichimoku Cloud).
- Triangle Trading Patterns.

When there are higher nadirs in addition to stable peaks, this recommends to traders that it is undergoing a duration of combination. Debt consolidation generally takes place before a major cost swing (which in this situation, would be adverse). Finding out about triangle trading as well as various other geometric trading strategies, will make you a better swing investor.

This swing trading sign is made up of 3 moving standards:

- The main moving standard, which is a straightforward moving standard.
- And then on both sides of these straightforward relocating averages are outlined two other relocating standards at a distance of 2 standard deviations away from the main moving average.

The number above should provide you a great depiction of what Bollinger Bands resemble. Most trading platforms come with this indication in their default list of indicato1rs.

The preferred setup for the swing trading sign is the default setups since it makes our signals more purposeful. We reached this final thought after evaluating the technique based upon a number of inputs.

Currently, let's move forward to the most important part of this chapter, the trading guidelines of the swing trading approach that works.

Prior to we go any better, we always suggest jotting down the trading rules on a notepad. This exercise will step up your learning curve and you'll come to be a swing trader expert in no time at all.

Swing Trading Method That Actually Works

This approach is actually simply comprised of 2 components. The first component of any kind of swing technique that works is an access filter. For the entrance filter, we're going to use one of the favoured swing trading indications aka the Bollinger Bands. The second aspect is a price action-based approach.

Step # 1: Wait for the price to touch the upper Bollinger Band.

The first component we want to see for our straightforward trading method is that we need to see stock cost moving right into the overbought region. Any swing trading technique that works should have this element included.

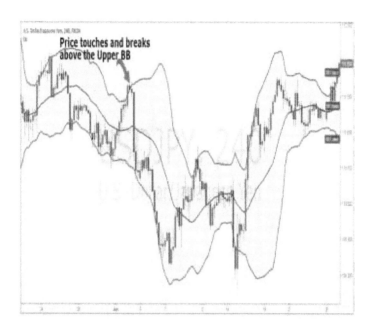

Note: The favored time frame for this simple swing trading approach is the 4h timespan. This method can likewise be made use of on a day-to-day and weekly period also.

Step # 2: Wait for the cost to Break listed below the Middle Bollinger Bands.

After we have actually touched the upper Bollinger Band, we want to see confirmation that we are in overbought area and also the marketplace is about to turn around. The rational filter, in this case, is to look after a break listed below the middle Bollinger Band.

This break below center Bollinger Bands is a clear signal in the shift in market view.

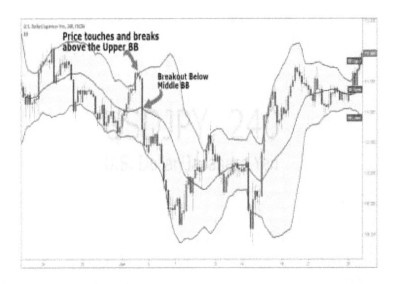

Step # 3: Swing Trading Indicator: The Breakout candle requires to large a Big Bold candle that closes near the Low Range of the Candlestick.

Thus far our favored swing trading indication has properly predicted this sell-off, however we're going to make use of a really basic candlestick-based approach for our entrance trigger. For access, we intend to see a huge bold bearish candle light that damages listed below the center Bollinger Band.

The 2nd element of this candlestick-based method is that we require the breakout candle light to shut near the reduced series of the candlestick. This is a measure of strong sellers, which actually want to drive this money pair much reduced.

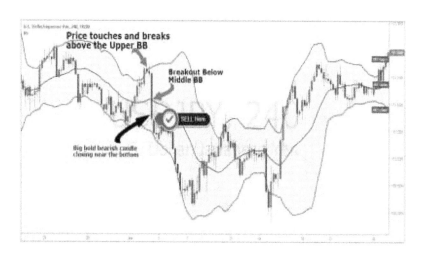

Every swing technique that works demands to have rather straightforward access filters. Currently, we still require to specify where to put our safety quit loss as well as where to take profits, which brings us to the following action of our basic swing trading approach.

Action # 4: We hide our Protective Stop Loss over the Breakout Candle.

The outbreak candle has a great deal of value because we've used it in our candlestick-based access approach. We thought that this candle light reveals the visibility of genuine vendors in the market. If the high of this candle were to be broken, it's clear enough that this is just a phony breakout as there are no actual sellers.

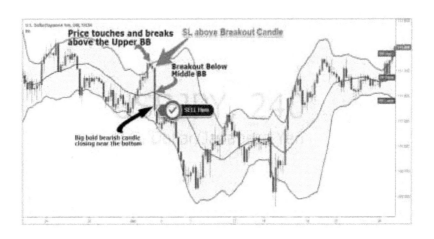

The next part of our easy swing trading approach is the departure technique which is based upon our favored swing trading indicator.

Action # 5: Take Profit once we break and also close back over the center Bollinger Bands.

In this specific case, we're looking at a brief trading example. So, if the cost breaks back over the middle Bollinger Banks it's time to get worried as well as take our earnings as it can indicate a reversal.

The reason why we take profit right here is rather easy to understand. We want to book the profits at the very early indicator the marketplace is ready to roll over.

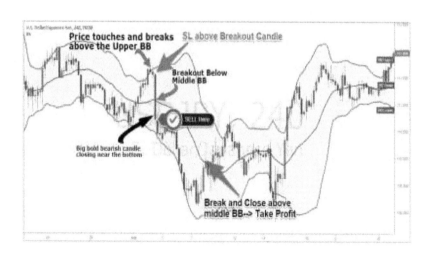

Note* The above was an example of a SELL profession. Utilize the exact same rules however backwards for a BUY profession.

In the number listed below, you can see a real BUY profession example, utilizing our easy swing trading strategy.

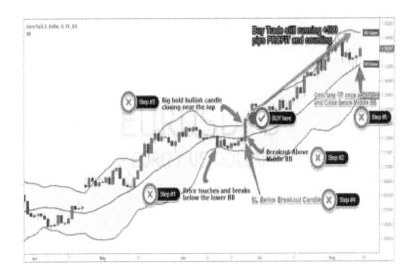

CHAPTER TEN

Automated Stock Trading Software

Research has showed that lot of people faces challenges when choosing the very best software that can be used for trading. This chapter will discuss the Information you need to evaluate stock trading software.

In today's market, investors are asking if they need to even buy stocks as well as if they can generate income. The solution to both is "yes." Stock market trading is a terrific chance currently, with costs lower as well as volatility higher than in years.

There are many automated trading platforms of robotic trading programs, on the internet, the best way to define the supply trading systems that can help you to make a supply financial investment and to expand your cash. Review the criteria below and recognize your own personal preferences by speaking with other stock traders. Identify the truths you need to compare programs. You'll need a good understanding of the automated trading devices' features as well as expenses before you make a decision.

Lots of kinds of firms provide stock trading suggestions as well as stock trading methods. They run the gamut from educational programs that aim to teach you how to trade, to a listing of suggested supplies to deal at specific triggers, to broker agent firm proprietary software program, all the way to completely automated robotic software. Costs can vary from hundreds of dollars to less than $50 a month for some automobile trading software. This chapter will direct you via the functions and advantages of the programs that are available for online supply trading. A lot of the programs are geared in the direction of "day investors," that practically open lengthy settings (buy) or short positions (sell short) as well as shut these settings the exact same day. Not everyone that utilizes these programs closes out their settings by the end of the trading day-- occasionally they hold their placements for days, weeks or months. We'll call this "energetic trading." Sometimes this is also referred to as "swing trading."

The essential functions of a supply trading program consist of an information feed for supply quotes and indicators, stock charts or charting ability of major indications, current balance and settings and an order entrance system. The order access system should enable quit (loss) orders, quit limit orders and tracking stops. A tracking stop limit is similar to the quit (loss), other than its loss will certainly be measured from the supplies highest point attained. The favored method would certainly be to keep the trigger costs in stealth setting, not viewable by the market makers, instead of as real orders. A lot of automated trading software ought to include a watch checklist of the supplies to possibly trade based upon the specifications the supply investor has actually gotten in.

Exchange Traded Funds (ETF's) can be part of a reliable trading technique. These are mutual funds that are traded intraday on the stock market, unlike typical mutual funds that are a basket of safeties valued at the close of the marketplace. On-line supply trading systems need to likewise consist of trading capabilities for ETF's.

Other features to search for include safety measures that supply traders may take, such as establishing a profit objective, the minimal price rise an investor would certainly anticipate a supply to gain before shutting their setting. Additionally, highly preferable is a kind of profit defense for your financial investments, which is the lower revenue goal. After the stock reaches its earnings objective and remains to increase, the supply trading software application must wait and also allow the profit rise. If the stock cost lowers or pulls back, the on the internet trading program need to shut the placement and also secure the profit. This pullback worth ought to not have any type of result before the profit goal is reached as well as is intended to improve supply performance. Extra innovative car trading programs will certainly additionally provide the percentage gain from the supply trader's access rate, as well as the investor can also specify a minimal quantity in case the portion gained is too reduced.

Inspect the Features and also Ask Questions

Number of Technical Indicators

There are actually numerous indicators that supply investors can make use of to determine which stocks to deal as well as when. The most durable programs will certainly use numerous indications for technical evaluation, such as Bollinger Bands, as well as some will certainly even consist of indications for Candlestick Chart developments. Robot programs use these indicators to establish conditions under which on-line investing will happen.

Intricacy

Automated stock trading programs differ greatly in ease of use. Some online stock trading systems do require real programming knowledge. Take a look at the online demo to see that it fits your level of comfort before making any commitment. Speak to others that are currently using the automated trading sites and check them up on the internet for more comments.

Variety of Long as well as Short Strategies Per Account

Due to the size of the online trading platform, there may be a restriction on the variety of techniques that you can have filled on each account. If you wish to run, claim two lengthy trading methods, then you may require two accounts. Additionally, validate if you have enough memory on your computer system for two or even more accounts. Experienced energetic investors might run two or more real-time long and short methods while having extra make up techniques that they are evaluating in a simulator setting.

Advised Additional Features

The finest automated supply trading software will certainly consist of additional functions that energetic investors will locate indispensable once they have actually begun computerized trading.

Additional strategy and also order access functions consist of the ability to add to a position as a stock rises, or as the stock declines, in addition to a minimal acquisition interval that the stock price should go down prior to it begins buying added shares. A maximum bid/ask range will also be handy, as the size of the spread can straight influence a swing investor's ability to make profitable professions.

If there are hundreds of indicators, as is the case with robot traders, see if the definitions of the signs are easily offered. The meaning or formula for signs may vary from one electronic trading system to another, so make sure you understand them first.

Advise you have a program that presents existing Profit and also Loss (P&L) on your employment opportunities and also the standing of the rules on your watch list. For instance, if a supply on the watch listing hasn't traded, exists a feature where the investor can bring up the regulations and signs to see which one(s) is stopping the profession?

Some automated stock trading programs aesthetically present the portion of icons up and down in each industry from the defined period to the present time so you can see exactly how the marketplace is transforming. Does the system include the capability to obstruct certain symbols from trading? If you're running a lengthy trading approach, you won't intend to be buying ETF's that short the market.

Day traders will want automatic trading software that tracks and also presents the number of day trades continuing to be. Day trading is controlled by the SEC, so it's crucial to comprehend if you will be day trading initially.

Orders in Stealth Mode

A basic function of many trading software programs is the capability to get in restriction, quit as well as quit limit orders. While it is important to have an exit strategy from your placements, telegraphing it to the institutional investors in the form of publicly watched limits is not. It's a little like poker, whoever can see all the hands has the advantage. Instead, more recent programs enable the user to go into these price points in the auto trader system, however trigger a market order when the problems are fulfilled. This is one advantage of a robotic stock trading program.

Instantly Executes Your Trading Strategy Even While You're Away From Your Computer

Very few couple of securities market trading systems can in fact do this. For those that do, it's done based upon the investor picking technical indications, comparison operators and also mathematical inputs that will certainly trigger opening, contributing to, or shutting stock settings. Essentially, it's a regulations driven software application system. The trader can select from numerous historic indicators representing the supplies' previous conditions.

The signs need to be updated daily using the latest data. Programs that can trade automatically are the lotion of the online spending software application crop. They take the emotion out of investing. Long period of time traders report that the simplest techniques, when delegated run on their very own for long periods do finest. The program must also have a manual override so the stock investor can manually position a trade as well. Specifically ask if the system has this capacity. Several market themselves as "automated trading" yet are not genuinely automated.

Capability to Simulate Strategies In Real Time Before Running Live

Most traders would certainly agree that they 'd such as to "check drive" a system before utilizing it. Some programs allow this with "back-testing," in which the program uses past data to implement the professions as well as show you what they would certainly have been. This is not always precise, as there is much information needed to perform a detailed back-test as well as it's nearly difficult to duplicate all the circumstances with simply the historical information. On top of that, how the system performed in a market last month or in 2015 does not show just how it will certainly perform in the here and now.

There are a couple of systems that allow the stock trader to replicate strategies, yet this is done mainly with paper tickets, as opposed to with the software. The best supply trading software program will let you exercise supply trading utilizing an online real-time data feed during market hours.

This is the preferred method, as it gives traders an extremely sensible sight of how their trading strategy is executing as well as the capacity to really feel the low and high of day-to-day trading without investing genuine money. If you can imitate professions, you won't need to open an actual brokerage account until you go "live" with actual cash. Ask if there is a limit on how long you can run in the simulation mode.

Reveals You How to Create A Stock Trading Strategy

There ought to be a step by step go through to show newbie traders exactly how to create a trading technique. Are there off-the-shelf techniques that are offered for your usage? Exist any costs included or are they supplied completely free? Can you modify the off the shelf methods? Keep in mind that firms should not be ensuring you a certain return. The very best companies will have long and also brief supply trading strategies readily available at on the house as well as will certainly enable the stock investor to create their own. Some companies will also enable you to duplicate strategies from a "buddies" checklist. One dimension does not fit all. If the company doesn't inform you the details of the strategy or why they selected or advise a certain stock, after that it's not suggested to utilize it. You may be paying too much for "proprietary" services and also may have the ability to obtain free securities market pointers and suggestions online that will do comparably.

Technology Support and Customer Service

The best automated stock trading software program firms have a very high "up-time" and also are extremely rarely out of service. Look at the company's document, just how commonly have they had failures? The software application needs to be simple to set up and also should work with a selection of running systems (Windows XP, Windows Vista, and so on). If you have inquiries, is there an experienced and also helpful personnel to provide solution? Just how promptly do they respond, if by email?

Compensations

Trading payments can eat into your earnings if you are not careful regarding picking a strategy that fits your demands. Compensations can differ greatly from broker to broker, relying on the number of shares traded, whether the shares are in rounded lots of 100, cost of the shares traded as well as the variety of trades you put every month.

Stock traders might also want to have more than one account if they have a trading method that typically trades 100 shares whole lots and also one more that trades 1000 share great deals. It pays to read the fine print.

Variety Of Broker Options

If you have an exclusive broker agent software, then you'll only have the ability to trade with that firm. The best online trading consists of the most affordable compensations for the normal professions for every technique that you utilize. There are various other programs whose software program has been incorporated into the order putting functionality at a selection of broker agent companies.

Compensations will certainly be one consideration in picking a company. Another is the margin rates. If you pick to have a margin account as well as borrow against the value of your protections to open a lot more placements, you will certainly be billed margin passion. Prices will vary by company. Commonly, companies with the most affordable commissions will not pay you passion or provide a cash market fund for your unvested cash. This is just how they maintain their prices down. If you anticipate having additional cash money that you will not make use of for trading, you might intend to keep it in an additional account where it can gain much more. You should also inspect if there is a minimum to open an account or a minimum number of trades called for.

Examine the Costs and also Software Support

Initial Software Fee and Monthly Fees - Ask exists is a preliminary charge to get the software. Is it countless dollars? If so, find out what you are really obtaining. Much of what you can obtain from a few of these programs can be located in cost-effective publications or on the Internet completely free. Is there likewise a month-to-month fee? If so, what does it cover? In assessing on-line trading solutions, more expensive software is not necessarily far better. Some energetic investing services are less expensive because they have more clients.

Information Feed Fee - Does the program consist of real time data feeds for stock quotes as well as signs? Exists an extra charge for this or is it consisted of in the fundamental monthly fee? This is the most significant component price in developing computerized stock trading programs. Or, is the information delayed by 20 minutes? Is it just the end of day information? If so, also in a simulation, old information is bad data.

Many brokerage firm companies supply cost-free Level II prices quote to certified energetic traders who trade a defined variety of professions monthly.

Supply Charts Fee - How will you examine the significant indications that you're making use of to make trading choices? Some programs include stock charts with their fee, others charge a different cost for it. Depending on the platform you select, you may or might not require a charting package. Figure out how much is it and just how much you can customize the supply charts to track your preferred indicators.

Ongoing Support Fee - Ask is there are any other fees. Covert costs will certainly each into a stock trader's earnings. If you're not in the marketplace to generate income, after that you should not be in the market.

Long-term Contract - Is the fee you're paying in advance for a year's contract? If so, is it instantly restored every year?

Training Fee - Find out if there is a separate training cost. For programs that market themselves as monetary instructors, there will be a charge, in some cases hundreds or countless bucks, as this is exactly how they make their cash. The most effective automated supply trading software application give free training.

Educating Formats - Is the training in the form of a real-time seminar? Webinar? Exist extra materials such as DVD's that you must buy to figure out all the information marketed? Or, is online training readily available in the business's office?

Minimum to Invest - Brokerage companies have their own minimums however there are additionally account minimal balances required by the Securities and Exchange Commission (SEC) wherefore it calls "pattern day traders." A day profession occurs when a trader opens as well as closes the same setting in a margin account on the very same day.

A pattern day trader is anybody who implements 4 or more day trades within 5 service days in a margin account, supplied the number of day trades is greater than 6% of the complete trades in the account throughout that duration. All pattern day traders should maintain a minimum of $25,000 in equity in any way times.

System Requirements –
The more durable the trading system, the higher the memory requirements. Examine this before you register or acquire a new computer. If you enroll in more than one account, will your

maker have sufficient RAM to run both or will you need to buy an additional computer system or more memory? If you have a Mac, ask if the software program works on Mac, as not all do. You might want to have actually one computer system devoted only to your automatic stock trading programs and also not run other word processing or spreadsheet programs.

Reports - The best automated stock trading software application will include a records function, that enables the stock trader to bring up trades by timespan, protection, lengthy vs brief, open vs. closed as well as P&L. For truly energetic investors, this information is a very easy method to track trading for tax obligation objectives.

Trading Strategy Statistics- In addition to Reports, another terrific feature is strategy data. They will certainly inform the very serious stock investor the number of trades carried and provide details in line with how profitable or unprofitable the trades have over different periods or intervals. Evaluating the approach accuracy raises the chances that a stock trader will certainly pay.

Online Trading Community - Trading system programmers who are really proud of their work welcome comments and also concerns from individuals. Take some time to review their supply trading forum and see what other stock investors are stating. There are even a few automatic stock trading programs that will take requests for additional indications from their users.

Take the Right Steps as You Choose Stock Trading Software

Be wary of those that inform you that you need to follow their stock trading system using only their devices. This has to do with you having control over your economic future. There are as numerous successful supply trading approaches as there are energetic traders. Experiment, speak with others and also do research. You will find what jobs best for you.

Usage caution when signing up for anything long-term, even if a 30-day cost-free test is offered. Some companies might ask for a big deposit or full payment ahead of time and also stress you instantly, guaranteeing a price cut if you join immediately. Some customers have reported problem in obtaining reimbursements even when they have complied with the procedures specifically.

CHAPTER ELEVEN

Technical And Fundamental Analysis

Technical analysis is the research study of the rate motion on a chart of a particular Forex money pair or other market. We can consider technological analysis or "T.A." for brief, as a sort of framework that investors make use of to study as well as utilize the price activity of a market.

The primary factor that investors use T.A. is to make forecasts concerning future rate motion based on past cost activity.

Technical analysts think that all present market variables are mirrored using the cost motion or price activity on a rate chart. So, if our team believe that all market variables are shown using cost activity, it only most likely to reason that we don't really require much else to evaluate and also trade the marketplaces besides cost. Being a technical expert and so are the participants in my trading neighborhood, we choose T.A. since we agree with the idea that all market variables are reflected using rate action, so we see no factor to make use of other ways to examine or trade the marketplace. That's not to say having some knowledge of basics as well as information occasions is a poor point, but we simply do not rely on them heavily.

Technical experts look for patterns on the graph that tend to duplicate themselves; they do this to develop their trading edge. The underlying reasoning here is that given that many price movements is driven by humans, certain patterns will certainly repeat themselves on the market as human beings often tend to be recurring in their emotion as well as communication with the market.

Technical analysis likewise encompasses discovering to examine the marketplace framework, discover trends, support, and resistance degrees and also typically discover to 'read' the ups and downs of a market. There is certainly discretion entailed right here and I will certainly be the first individual to tell you that T.A. is even more of an art than a science.

That said, it is something you will certainly get even more comfy with as well as far better at provided time as well as practice. T.A. forms the back-bone of major core trading method of cost action, which is merely a derivative or off-shoot of 'traditional T.A.", other than with even more clearness and shorter methods that do not include complicated foreign exchange indicators or points like Elliot Wave Theory that are much too messy and also open to interpretation for me to believe they are worth trading or training.

A lot of investors instantly think about a price graph like the one above when somebody discusses words "technical analysis." Rate charts provide us with a fantastic amount of beneficial data that paints a complete photo of a market's historical and current supply and need scenario, as well as the price levels that the market participants have actually regarded the most essential. As technical experts we require to pay special interest to these price levels as rate will certainly have a tendency to value them again and again; undoubtedly, a lot of my cost activity trading program is built around learning to identify and trade cost activity setups from vital degrees in the market. Price graphs are likewise a representation of all market individuals' ideas about the marketplace and also market variables, so by focusing your evaluation and trading on a market's cost graph you can streamline your trading and at the same time evaluate the end outcome of every little thing that contributes to the price motion of a market.

Fundamental Analysis

It is the study of how global economic information, as well as various other news events, affect economic markets. Fundamental evaluation encompasses any news event, social pressure, financial news, policy change, firm earnings as well as information, and also possibly one of the most essential piece.

Fundamental information suitable to the Forex market, which is a country's interest rates and rate of interest plan.

The suggestion behind fundamental analysis is that if a country's existing or future economic picture is strong, their money needs to enhance. A solid economic climate draws in foreign financial investment as well as organizations, and this suggests foreigners must purchase a nation's money to spend or start a service there. So, basically, everything boils down to supply and also demand; a country with a solid as well as expanding economic climate will experience more powerful need for their currency, which will work to decrease supply as well as increase the worth of the currency.

For example, if the Australian economic climate is gaining strength, the Australian dollar will certainly boost in worth relative to various other currencies. One primary reason a nation's currency ends up being more valuable as its economy grows and strengthens is due to the fact that a country will commonly elevate rate of interest to control development and inflation. Greater rate of interest is eye-catching to international investors and as a result they will certainly need to get Aussie dollars in order to purchase Australia, this certainly will certainly increase the need as well as rate of the money as well as reduce the supply of it.

Major financial occasions in Forex

Now, allows promptly review a few of one of the most important financial occasions that drive Forex rate motion. This is simply to familiarize you with some even more of the jargon that you will likely discover on your forex trip, you don't need to fret excessive concerning these financial events besides being aware of the moments they are released every month, which can be located each day in my Forex profession setups commentary.

The Gross Domestic Product (GDP).

The GDP record is just one of the most essential of all financial indicators. It is the largest action of the overall state of the economy. The GDP number is released at 8:30 am EST on the last day of each quarter as well as it shows the previous quarter's activity. The GDP is the accumulation (total amount) monetary worth of all the goods and also solutions generated by the whole economic climate throughout the quarter being determined; this does not include international task nevertheless. The growth rate of GDP is an important number to look for.

Trade Balance.

Trade balance is a procedure of the difference in between imports and also exports of tangible products and services. The degree of a nation's trade balance and also modifications in exports vs. imports is widely complied with and an important indicator of a nation's overall financial strength. It's much better to have even more exports than imports, as exports aid expand a nation's economic climate and reflect the general health and wellness of its production field.

Consumer Price Index (CPI).

The CPI record is the most extensively utilized procedure of rising cost of living. This report is released at 8:30 am EST around the 15th of monthly and it shows the previous month's information. CPI determines the modification in the price of a bundle of consumer goods and services from month to month

The Producer Price Index (PPI).

Together with the CPI, the PPI is among the two crucial procedures of inflation. This report is released at 8:30 am EST during the second complete week of every month and it reflects the previous month's data. The manufacturer, consumer price index, gauges the rate of goods at the wholesale level. So to comparison with CPI, the PPI gauges just how much manufacturers are getting for the goods while CPI determines the cost paid by consumers for goods.

Work Indicators.

The most vital employment news happens on the very first Friday of monthly at 8:30 am EST. This statement consists of the joblessness price; which is the percent of the workforce that is out of work, the number of brand-new work produced, the average hours functioned weekly, and also typical hourly revenues. This record frequently leads to substantial market movement. You will certainly typically listen to traders and analysts talking about "NFP", this indicates Non-Farm Employment record, and it is maybe the one record monthly that has the greatest power to relocate the marketplaces.

Consumer Goods Orders.

The durables orders record gives a dimension of just how much people are investing in longer-term purchases, these are defined as items that are anticipated to last more than 3 years. The report is released at 8:30 am EST around the 26th of every month and also is thought to give some understanding right into the future of the manufacturing industry.

Retail Sales Index.

The Retail Sales Index gauges products marketed within the retail sector, from large chains to smaller sized local shops, it takes a sampling of a collection of retail stores throughout the country. The Retail Sales Index is released at 8:30 am EST around the 12th of the month; it shows information from the previous month. This record is typically changed relatively dramatically after the last numbers appeared.

Real estate Data.

Housing data consists of the variety of new houses that a nation began building that month as well as existing house sales. Residential construction activity is a significant root cause of economic stimulus for a nation and so it's extensively followed by Forex individuals. Existing residence sales are a good measure of financial stamina of a country as well; reduced existing residence sales and reduced new house starts are typically an indication of a slow or weak economic climate.

Rate of interest.

Interest rates are the main driver in Forex markets; the Federal open market committee carefully watches every one of the above discussed financial indications to determine the general health and wellness of the economy. The Federal can make use of the devices at its disposable to lower, increase, or leave rate of interest unmodified, depending upon the evidence it has collected on the health and wellness of the economy. So while interest rates are the main chauffeur of Forex price action, every one of the above economic indicators are additionally very important.

Relationship between Technical Analysis and Fundamental Analysis.

Technical evaluation and Fundamental analysis are the two major schools of assumed in trading and investing in financial markets. Technical analysts consider the price motion of a market as well as use this details to make forecasts about its future rate direction. Basic analysts look at financial news, also referred to as fundamentals. Now, given that almost any type of worldwide news event can have an effect on globe financial markets, practically any type of information event can be financial news. This is an important point that I intend to make which many essential experts appear to neglect.

One of the primary reasons most members choose to trade primarily with technical evaluation is because there are essentially numerous different variables on the planet that can influence monetary markets at any one time. Currently, Forex is much more affected by macro events like a country's rates of interest plan or GDP numbers, however various other major news events like battles or all-natural calamities can likewise cause the Forex market to move. Hence, since I and also many others think that every one of these globe occasions are factored right into price as well as conveniently noticeable by analyzing it, there is merely no reason to attempt and also follow all the economic information occasions that take place each day, in order to trade the markets.

Among the main disagreements that I have actually checked out that essential experts have against technical analysts is that past cost information can not predict or aid predict future price activity, and also instead you have to make use of future or upcoming information (fundamentals) to predict the price activity of a market.

So, I believed it would be a good suggestion to provide my reaction to these two arguments versus technical analysis:

1. If essential experts wish to attempt as well as tell me that past rate data is not important, after that I would like them to describe to me why straight degrees of assistance and resistance are significant. I would additionally such as to inquire exactly how myself and also many various other rate activity investors can effectively trade the markets by discovering to trade off of a handful of

straightforward yet strongly anticipating price action signals:

Any type of Fundamental expert, that intends to claim that charts do not matter, is merely wrong, and you will concern this conclusion by yourself when you invest even more time researching some price charts.

2. The next debate that Fundamental analysts utilize is that you can more accurately forecast a market's rate movement by evaluate approaching foreign exchange news events. Well, anyone that has actually traded for any size of time recognizes that markets typically and generally react contrary to what an impending news occasion suggests. Are there times when the marketplace moves in the instructions indicated by an information occasion? Yes, absolutely, but is it something you can develop a trading method and trading strategy around? No.

The factor is that markets operate assumptions of the future. This is actually an approved fact of trading and also investing, so it's a little strange to me that some individuals still neglect technological analysis or don't largely concentrate on it when assessing as well as trading the markets. Let me discuss: if Non-farm payrolls is coming out (the most essential economic record each month, launched in the U.S.) as well as the marketplace is anticipating 100,000 even more tasks added last month, the marketplace will likely already have relocated anticipation of this number.

So, if the real number is 100,000 also, the marketplace will most likely relocate lower, rather than higher given that there were not more added tasks than anticipated. So, while 100,000 new tasks might be a great number, the fact that the actual record did not go beyond expectations is bad for traders as well as capitalists.

Since every one of the coming before assumptions of a news release have actually currently been carried out and show up on the price chart, why not just analyze and also discover to compromise the price activity on the rate chart?

You see, also after the news is released we can still make use of technical evaluation to trade the cost movement, so truly technical evaluation is the clearest, most practical, and also many valuable methods to analyze and also trade the markets. Am I claiming there is no space for Fundamental evaluation in a Forex investor's device box? Absolutely not.

However, what I am saying is that it must be checked out and also utilized as a praise to technological analysis as well as it need to be conserved, when doubtful consult the charts as well as read the price action, just utilize Fundamentals to sustain your Technical sight or out of pure inquisitiveness, never depend only on Fundamentals to forecast or trade the markets.

CHAPTER ELEVEN

Price Action Trading Analysis

Price activity analysis is the act of researching, checking out and also interpreting the cost movement of a market in time, which includes the use of raw cost graphs to trade the market (no signs). By learning to check out the price activity of a market, we can figure out a market's directional prejudice along with profession from persisting cost activity patterns or rate activity arrangements that show adjustments or continuations in market belief.

In easier terms: Price action analysis is the use of the all-natural or "raw" rate movement of a market to examine and also trade it. This indicates, you are making all of your trading decisions based purely on the price bars on a "naked" or indicator-free price chart.

All economic variables create rate activity which can be conveniently seen on a market's cost chart. Whether an economic variable is filtering system down through a human investor or a computer system trader, the movement that it creates in the market will certainly be quickly visible on a price graph. As a result, rather than trying to analyze a million financial variables each day (this is difficult certainly), you can simply find out to trade from cost action evaluation because this style of trading permits you to quickly assess as well as utilize all market variables by just reviewing as well as trading off of the cost activity created by stated market variables.

How to apply price activity evaluation to the Forex market?

First, price activity analysis can be made use of to trade any type of monetary market, given that it merely utilizes the "core" cost data of the marketplace. Nevertheless, my personal favorite market to trade is the Forex market, mostly as a result of its deep liquidity that makes it easy to get in as well as leave the marketplace, as well as also because the forex market often tends to have better trending problems in addition to even more volatility which makes for much better directional trading and also enables price activity trading to truly beam.

My personal method to trading and also training cost action trading is that you can trade properly from a few tried and true price action arrangements. There is no need to try and trade from 25 different price patterns, the Forex market moves in a fairly predictable fashion a lot of the time, so all we need is a handful of reliable rate action entrance configurations to provide us a good chance at finding as well as entering high-probability professions.

The first thing you require to do to apply price activity to the Forex market, is to strip your charts of all indicators as well as get a "tidy" rate chart with just the price bars in a shade you such as. I select easy black and white or blue as well as red for my colors, but you can pick whichever shades you like.

Right here's an instance of my day-to-day graph arrangement on the EURUSD:

A clean and simple price action chart

Now, let's consider an instance of a clean as well as straightforward rate chart next to a cost chart covered with several of the most prominent signs that numerous traders utilize. I want you to consider these two charts and consider which one seems easier and also much more sensible to compromise of:

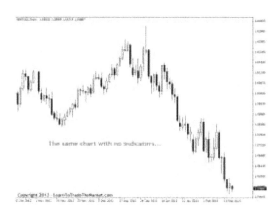

From looking at the two graphs above, you will possibly agree that it seems a little ridiculous to conceal the all-natural price activity of a market with unpleasant and also complex signs. All indicators are stemmed from rate motion anyways, so if we have a solid method to trade based just on rate motion (price action evaluation), it just makes good sense that we would utilize that rather than attempting to evaluate unpleasant additional data.

Price Activity Trading Signal

Next off, allows talk about exactly how we can use rate action analysis to locate access right into the Forex market from a raw price graph. As a result of years of trading the markets I have simplified all I have actually discovered right into my own distinct approach of trading with rate activity. This technique consists of a handful of very specific cost activity entrance activates that can offer you with a high-probability access right into the market. Essentially, what we are seeking is persisting price patterns that tell us something regarding what the marketplace could carry out in the near-future.

For purposes of brevity and also out of respect for my paid participants, I will not hand out every one of my trading techniques as well as access causes here, yet you can learn more regarding the trading approaches that I show in my trading training course. In the chart below, we are most likely to take a look at a specifically excellent price action signal for trading with trends; the within bar technique.

In the instance graph below, we can see one cost activity trading signal that I like to use in trending markets; the within bar configuration:

In an up-trending market like this we can watch for inside bar buy setups to trade in-line with the trend as they are often good continuation signals in a trending market...

inside bar

Inside bars

Copyright 2013 - LearnToTradeTheMarket.com

How to utilize cost action evaluation to establish a market's trend

You will possibly come across several signs developed to tell you what the trend of a market is. Nonetheless, the most reliable and relied on way for identifying a market's trend is merely to consider the daily charts and analyze the market's cost activity. To identify a sag, we search for patterns of reduced highs and also lower lows, often annotated by "LH as well as LL". To determine an uptrend, we seek patterns of higher highs and also higher lows, often annotated by "HH and HL". In the example chart below, we can see examples of a drop, an uptrend and an uptrend altering to a drop:

Where as well as when should you trade a cost action signal?

In my trading training course, I concentrate heavily on teaching my members exactly how to trade with "convergence". When I state "trading with assemblage" I am generally referring to looking for areas or degrees on the market that are clearly significant. Convergence indicates when points integrated or converge. Therefore, when we are wanting to "patronize confluence" we are trying to create an obvious rate activity signal with a considerable level in the marketplace. There are different aspects of confluence that we can look for, but in the graph listed below I am revealing you price action setups that created at essential assistance and resistance levels out there; support as well as resistance are each a factor of assemblage. Note, I have shown you 2 even more cost activity configurations in the chart listed below; the pin bar strategy and also the fake trading signal.

In the instance chart below, we are looking exactly how to trade price action configurations from confluent levels out there:

This lesson provided you a standard summary of what rate activity analysis is as well as just how to use it in the markets. From here, you must proceed to the following part of this novice's program and also continue learning about Forex and price action trading. As constantly, if you have any concerns regarding trading just email me below, as well as if you wish to learn more about how to patronize rate activity then checkout my rate action trading program for even more details.

Guide to Forex Trading Strategies for Beginners

You are not going to need to have a vast as well as in-depth understanding of the cash markets or business as well as economic market sectors if you want to become a Forex investor.

All that you will need is a forex trading account, a bankroll and also the capability of properly forecasting whether one currency is most likely to relocate value against any other currency.

When you begin trading forex online you are merely most likely to have to presume whether the money of any type of one country is going to relocate value, either upwards or downloads, versus any other money of your very own finding over any provided amount of time.

If the value of the money moves in the direction you predicted at the factor when your trade ends, then you have actually won as well as have earned a profit.

Opening a Forex Trading Account

To begin trading Forex on-line merely go to the website of any of trusted listed Forex Brokers and register as a new trader. It is going to take you less than a min to register as a new trader and also by doing so you will certainly after that have accessibility to two different kinds of trading accounts.

The initial kind of account we suggest you use as well as make full use is a trial trading account. That account will after that permit you to experiment with every one of the option setups on that particular trading platform and you will certainly be issued with an established number of totally free, no danger trading demonstration credit ratings.

You are then able to position those demo credit scores on absolutely any of the real-time trading possibilities offered to you. By placing a series of various professions, you will certainly soon master exactly how to put professions, the framework of each kind of profession and exactly how those trades work and also operate.

As soon as you have grasped the art of using a trading system you will certainly then be able to switch over to utilizing a genuine money trading account.

Selecting the Trades You Can Place

If you have decided to open a demonstration trading account as recommended, then you will possibly have placed your trades randomly with no assumption in regards to the two currencies you have paired against each other.

However, when you are trading genuinely with your funds, you need to spend quite a long time in regards to which currencies you must pair together, as it will certainly be your cash that goes to risk on those trades.

The way in which you pair your professions likewise matters, for one of your options will certainly be the currency you wish to acquire in worth as well as the various other will certainly be the one which you are really hoping falls in value and also as such will certainly see you having actually earned a profit on those professions.

Keeping that in mind you require to be taking a look around for tools which are most likely to allow you to detect which currencies are likely to drop and also rise in value. Forex trading tools that are freely available to you, so do have a great look round our site.

Getting Lots of Trading Value

When you make any high valued acquisition, you are always most likely to search as well as contrast the cost of whatever it is you are seeking to purchase. This is constantly something that you must be doing when you are looking for a Forex Broker at which to subscribe to.

There are most likely to be an entire host of enticements available to you to subscribe to any Forex Broker, as well as those enticements are typically in the form of a reward which you are most likely to have the ability to assert when you register at a Broker and afterwards make a deposit into your account.

Keeping that in mind prior to you simply open up a Forex trading account at the very first Broker you find, invest as much time as is required looking into and comparing what each of them will offer you as a new trader, after that join to the one with the most generous as well as high valued new investor reward offer.

CHAPTER TWELVE

Common Trading Mistakes and Traps

There are common mistakes and 'traps' that offer nearly all investors trouble at some time in their trading jobs. So, let's cover one of the most usual blunders that traders make which keep them from making money on the market:

1. Analysis-paralysis

There is a practically unlimited amount of Forex news variables that can distract a trader, as well as heaps as well as lots of trading systems as well as trading software application. You'll need to filter with every one of these variables and forge a trading method that is basic yet effective, warning; this can be a really a difficult task for newbie traders.

The reason why, is that many investors appear to assume that 'a lot more is far better', when actually 'a lot more' is in fact worse, as it associates with Forex trading. There really is no requirement to sit in front of your computer for hours on end analyzing Foreign exchange news reports or many indicators.

2. Over-trading

Many investors do not generate income in the marketplace over the long-run for one basic factor: they trade method excessive. One curious reality of trading is that a lot of traders do effectively on trial accounts, yet after that when they begin trading real cash they do terribly. The reason for this is that in trial trading there is virtually no emotion involved because your real money is out the line. So, this most likely to show that emotion is the number 1 destroyer of trading success. Investors who over-trade are operating purely on feeling.

Trading when your pre-defined trading side is not really existing is over-trading. Trading if you have no trading plan or have not understood a trading edge yet is over-trading. Basically, you need to recognize precisely what you're seeking on the market and then ONLY trade when your edge exists.

Trading excessive causes you to acquire deal expenses (spreads or compensations), and it additionally causes you to lose money a great deal quicker because you are simply wagering in the marketplace. You require to take a calm and also computed approached to the marketplace, not a drunken-gamblers approach, which appears to be the popular method of many investors.

3. Not using danger benefit and finance appropriately

Risk monitoring is critical to attaining success in the marketplace. Risk administration entails managing your risk per trade to a level that is tolerable for you. Many traders overlook the fact that they could shed on any trade. If you recognize and accept that you might lose on any kind of profession, why would you ever take the chance of more than you fit with shedding? Yet traders make this error time and time again, the mistake of risking way too much money per trade. It just takes one over-leveraged profession that violates you to set off a chain of emotional trading errors that erases your trading account a lot faster than you believe.

4. No trading strategy and no regular or self-control

Not having a Forex trading strategy is probably the most common trading mistake the Foreign exchange investors make. Several traders seem to think that they will develop a trading strategy "later" or after they start making money or that they just do not need one or can simply keep it "in their heads". All of these rationalizations are merely maintaining traders from attaining the success they so terribly need.

If you do not have a Forex trading strategy that details all of your actions in the market along with your general trading approach and technique, you will certainly be far more most likely to operate emotionally and also from a gambling mindset. Beginner traders especially need a Forex trading strategy to solidify their trading technique as well as to produce a guide that they use to trade the marketplace from, and you cannot keep it in your head ... you need to physically draw up your trading plan as well as read it every day you trade.

5. Trading genuine cash ahead of time or gambling it

Need to dive into the market and also start trading real cash is often excessive for a lot of traders to hold up against. Nevertheless, the reality is that up until you have mastered an effective Forex trading approach like cost activity trading, you truly should not be trading real cash. By "understanding" the approach, I imply you need to be regularly effective with it on a demo make up a duration of 3 to 6 months or even more, before going real-time. Nonetheless, you do not want to make use of demonstration account trading as a crutch, trading a real account is different due to the genuine feelings involved, so just make sure you change to real-money trading after you have accomplished success on demonstration, don't be afraid of trading actual cash, since ultimately you will require to make the switch to real money trading.

CHAPTER THIRTEEN

Stock Market

The stock market is attracting a lot of traders on the day to day basis as it is characterized by many swings and fluctuations. These swings are the salt and pepper for traders as profits can be made. Exactly such swings are the reason why Forex market is so popular as well. If the market would be characterized by small movements, or mostly ranges, it will be difficult to capitalize on such moves and the trading concept would not be so widely accepted.

So far you should have an idea about what is driving the Forex market and what foreign exchange stays for. Some traders are still confused when looking for a market to trade and don't know what to trade: stocks or Forex.

Are these two markets equally risky? Is the approach the same or traders should consider different things when trading them?

Differences Between the Forex and Stock Market

There are some notable differences between the two markets and they must be mentioned here. From the brokers that offer the financial products to be traded, all the way to the factors that influence the markets… everything is different. Below there are the main factors that matter when trading both Forex and stocks. Please note that they are not listed based on their relevance, but simply because traders must know the difference between these markets.

1. The Way to Trade Them

The main difference between the two financial markets comes from the way they are traded. To be more exact, stock market trading has some limitations that are not seen on the Forex market. To start, when trading stocks, it is not possible to sell a stock, unless you already own it. This sounds only normal, but on the Forex market, one can sell a currency pair without owning it. In other words, you can go short EURUSD, for example, on the Forex market, and if the currency pair is moving South, you can bank on that move and make a profit by covering the short (hence closing the position with a long) at lower levels. This is not possible on the stock market. The only way to sell a stock is to own it. This means, you must buy it first, and if it moves against you, you can sell it but in a loss. If it moves up, you can sell it for a profit. But you must own it first, and this makes for different trading strategies to be in place for the stock and Forex market.

2. Brokers to Trade Them

You may find it difficult to believe, but there are few or little brokers that offer you the possibility to trade both Forex and stocks on the same trading account. Moreover, there is unlikely that a broker will offer both products. Therefore, it is either you trade stocks with a dedicated broker for the stock market, or you don't trade them at all. It means that to trade both stocks and Forex, you need to have trading accounts with two different entities, or brokerage houses. Margins needed for trading the two markets are different too. While the Forex market is known to be the most leveraged one, on the stock market a cash account is mostly used to cover the expenses when buying stocks. There are, though, stock brokers that offer margin trading as well, but this is not widespread as it is in the case of Forex trading. Moreover, costs are different when trading Forex and stocks, with the last one being more expensive.

Factors that Make the Two Markets Move

Like any financial product, supply and demand are governing the way the product is moving. If there is bigger volume one the long side, the product will move up and the other way around if the volume on the short side is bigger. Both markets are moving based on fundamental and technical factors. Fundamental analysis is news related. This means that when economic news, like unemployment rate, GDP (Gross Domestic Product), interest rates, retail sales, etc., is released, both markets are moving. However, they are not moving the same on fundamental analysis. Technical analysis, on the other hand, is based on interpreted previous patterns that formed back in time with the purpose of forecasting future price levels. No matter the financial product traded, technical analysis is the same. However, here we need to differentiate between two things: trading stocks and trading indices. An index is moving based on the aggregate move of the stocks that are being part of it. For example, the DJIA (Dow Jones Industrial Average) is formed out of thirty companies. Because of that, it is also being called Dow30. The way these thirty stock prices are moving will determine if the Dow Jones will end up higher or lower on any given day. However, the companies represented in the Dow are not having the same weight: some represent 0.5% of the whole index, other 1.7%, and so on. This makes it possible for the Dow to be positive if the heavily weighted companies in the index are green and the other ones red. And the other way around being true as well! There is an index for any stock market in the world, and these indices are being offered by Forex brokers as well, as an individual and separate financial product. Therefore, there's no need for having a separate trading account to trade indices.

However, there is not possible to trade one single stock on an index with a Forex trading account. If your broker says it is possible, think again: what the broker is offering for trading is a CFD (Contract for Difference) and not the real stock. For more about CFD's, please refer to the article dedicated to that subject here on our Trading Academy – Forex vs. CFDs. As a reminder, CFD's are one of the most riskier financial assets to be traded, and, as such, require considerable margin in the trading account. There are other factors that are different for the stock market when compared with the Forex one. One of such a factor is the earnings calendar.

On a quarterly basis, companies around the world are releasing their earnings, and traders are reacting to these releases by taking a position in a new company or simply closing a previous position. Moreover, in between these quarterly releases, stocks are being rated by analysts.

When these ratings are changing to different levels, from buy to neutral or sell, the price of an individual stock is changing. This is not happening on the Forex market, as the dynamics are simply different when compared with the stock market. Keep in mind that everything discussed here about stock and forex market is only a few things that differentiate the two. They are clearly distinct ones, and one should be aware of that before engaging in trading.

CHAPTER FOURTEEN

Commodities

The popularity of trading futures and options has been growing rapidly for several years. The ease of accessing constantly updated data online has prompted an increased fever by day traders to attempt to be successful and make money in this risky investment area. Individuals can now trade these markets with the same ease and speed as large companies.

In the United States, an individual, cannot trade futures contracts and options on futures contracts directly on an exchange. A person or firm must trade on your behalf. People and firms who trade on your behalf as a customer generally must be registered with the Commodity Futures Trading Commission.

Commodity Pool.

You might likewise trade commodities with a "asset pool." This suggests you are buying a share or passion in the pool, and also trades are implemented for the pool as a whole, rather than for the people who have a rate of interests in the pool. Commodity pool participants share in any type of gains or losses.

If you have a conflict or a trouble arises out of your commodity futures or option account, first attempt to settle the trouble with your broker. If that is not successful, then you have alternatives for fixing conflicts; the CFTC Reparations program and market funded adjudication; or court litigation.

In choosing a specific approach, you may wish to think about the cost, size of time involved and whether or not the assistance of a lawyer is needed. More info on dispute resolution is readily available from the CFTC's Office of Proceedings.

Correlation Between Commodities as well as Forex

Nonetheless, professional traders take one step further and also take into consideration every possible element which has the tendency to impact foreign exchange rates.

It is necessary to state that currency exchange rates are commonly relocated by factors like rates of interest, national politics, supply and also need, economic stability, commodity rates and also other associated aspects.

Even if you do not have the technological as well as in-depth understanding, you would still have actually listened to information related to oil cost movements and transform in money costs as a straight outcome of it. Assets like oil and also gold have a high correlation with particular money that has essentially stayed the very same throughout the years.

One of one of the most vital as well as standard things related to understanding the various variables that influence the foreign exchange market is comprehending just how different assets correlate with different currencies.

US Dollar and Gold Correlation

Different commodities have a tendency to have a various relationship with each currency. As an example, the relationship between the US Dollar (USD) and also Gold is typically inversely proportional, or as it's normally claimed gold and the USD are vice versa associated.

The logic here is that financiers have a tendency to rely on gold for their investments in times of economic trouble and increased threats of high rising cost of living.

Swiss Franc and Gold Relationship

On the other hand, the Swiss Franc (CHF) is favorably associated with gold costs because of the fact that like gold the Swiss money is regarded as a safe house by investors, and on top of that, a big quantity of Swiss currency books is backed by gold.

Canadian Buck as well as Oil Connection

The Canadian Dollar (CAD) is among those currencies which have a favorable connection with oil mostly due to the fact that Canada has the 2nd largest gets of oil, just after Saudi Arabia.

Canada also exports the majority of the oil it creates for this reason a rise in oil prices brings about a stronger demand for the Canadian Buck due to the fact that importers need to pay for Canadian oil with the Canadian currency.

Australian Dollar and Gold Relationship

Likewise, Australia is amongst the top five exporters of gold and also any type of rise in gold prices is likely to have a favorable impact on the Australian Buck (AUD).

Oil (black) and also upside down USDCAD (red) - Connection has actually been rather regular over the years

Oil (black) as well as upside down USDCAD (red) - Correlation has actually been fairly regular for many years

Analysis of inter-market possessions can be extremely complicated, so let's proceed with the instance of the Canadian Buck and oil prices to clarify this point. Canada's economic climate is hugely dependent on oil exports as we kept in mind earlier.

Much more importantly, a large section of its general exports, i.e. up to 85%, goes to the United States of America. Therefore, there might be no demand to evaluate international oil need because even if international oil need is regular, a massive increase in American oil need can pull up the oil prices in Canada, resulting in an appreciation of CAD.

For this reason, a mutual understanding of the economic situation of a particular nation and also numerous factors influencing demand as well as supply of underlying commodities is essential in order to guarantee reliable analysis.

When evaluating the inter-market correlation in between currencies and assets, one of the most effective techniques might be to focus on the Australian Dollar (AUD) and also its motions.

As talked about in an earlier paragraph, AUD has a strong favorable relationship with gold costs. Gold costs as well as the Australian Dollar rise and fall in a comparable manner. Thus, AUD can be utilized to recognize gold cost fads and also the other way around.

The typical relationship in between gold and also AUD is determined to be +0.51. Moreover, the Australian Buck is additionally understood to relocate tandem with the rate of crude oil, although the relationship is considerably less than with gold. The average correlation between oil and AUD has been estimated to be +0.23.

Some investors trade both products and also currencies simultaneously. The precise nature of this trading depends upon each private investor as well as his aspirations as well as risk cravings. As an example, two opposing instruments can be consisted of in a portfolio to reduce direct exposure to risk. As a matter of fact, a trader can likewise choose to consist of 2 positively correlated assets and money with the hope of increasing his earnings.

There is nothing wrong in taking either of these courses, however, each decision must be backed by logical reasoning as well as solid logics rather than mere instinct or assumptions.

The very best and also probably the simplest strategy, when determining to trade both assets as well as currencies concurrently, is to recognize the connection between them. Analyze past fads and see if they declare or adversely correlated over a certain time period. Discover if one commodity appears to be leading the various other and also the other way around.

While it holds true that inescapable correlation exists in between commodities and also currencies, still, it is important to bear in mind that connections are not equivalent every single time and also correlations can change.

Furthermore, a favorable correlation can even turn into adverse correlation for a brief time and vice versa. It is, therefore, strongly advised to always keep an eye on the existing level of relationship and examine if rates begin to diverge and also possibly lead to a failure of the relationship in between the two property courses.

Product trading as well as forex trading are the key approaches to trade and 2 of the marketplaces which are most comfortable to spend your cash. Several buyers pertain to forex and also commodity shares because of the low prices of shares in the supply market.

In line with the above, numerous investors are making their lot of money due to the use of these techniques. Nonetheless, asset trading and also foreign exchange trading have their advantages and downsides.

As stated above, trading in foreign exchange as well as assets has its benefits as well as disadvantages. So, capitalists frequently believe that forex trading is riskier than product trading. Investors who do not have good risk-bearing capacity often tend to like to trade in currency pairs.

Commodity trading is done by utilizing futures agreements. In this line, a futures agreement refers to a deal in between a customer and also vendor to offer or acquire a product at a specific rate on a specified future date.

Whereas, foreign exchange trading refers to practices of marketing and also purchasing of the currency. Money are traded on large financial institutions and large investors. So, foreign exchange or trading in money is taken into consideration to be one of the most liquid market around the globe.

Both commodity trading as well as forex trading often tend to be amazing as well as rewarding. However, it does not matter which sort of profession you intended to spend your cash. The concern of 'which one pays?' is important.

Consequently, it depends on the investor and also his/her trading approach to make a decision exactly how to make either forex or product trading successful.

Foreign exchange trading has even more details offered for foreign exchange trading, and also with the information being more economical or cost-free, total with free demo accounts, it is hard to fail with forex trading.

What affects both trades?

When traders buy commodities trading, they figure out if the cost of a details asset will increase or drop based upon whether they think there will be a good farming season.

A negative expanding season, enhanced mining prospects, dry spell, strikes or floods, and so on. Mother earth plays a really crucial function in trading commodities than it performs in trading foreign exchange. The unforeseeable weather condition patterns from year to year can impact adversely on the commodities market.

Also, if it's not the weather it could be new mineral explorations, completely dry holes, battle or a wide range of different events, strikes by miners every one of which can transform the outcomes for commodity trading.

Simply put, the possibility of good-sized profit exists in the products market. Nonetheless, there are higher possibilities of losses because of plant failures, and so on. As a result, traders require to be very careful if they believe to purchase asset trading.

Forex trading makes up whether a specific country's currency will certainly increase or drop compared to another major currency. When trading in the foreign exchange, capitalists trade money pairs, i.e., nationwide money sets which increase or fall relative to each other.

Consequently, foreign exchange trading can additionally be influenced by international modifications, however they commonly have a much less remarkable impact than what can occur with commodities. Seeing it from the point of view one can securely say forex trading is the safer bet of both.

Commodities might be simple to exchange because asset costs are normally based simultaneously on-demand and also supply.

For that reason, whatever traded concentrates mainly on supply as well as demand so its fad may be extra predictable. Whereas, forex might be smooth to trade if one utilizes the best trading equipment or technique.

Are there Earnings when trading commodities?

Commodity trading might be really lucrative; nevertheless, it mainly depends on the amount of money which one makes use of to begin spending.

Foreign exchange trading additionally can be a lot more lucrative. Capitalists have the option of trading with take advantage of. However also as trading with leverage is unpredictable, it enhances traders' capability to make revenues.

To summarize the above, it is essential to claim that the balance tip prefers forex trading. Nonetheless, traders should constantly choose based on their investment objectives and also strategies.

For that reason, speaking with and also learning more information would be handy in making the best choice.

Successful trading is straightforward, yet hard. It will need you to work hard, obtain the proper exchange training, and also discover to develop an effective frame of mind. You'll have start with the basics of foreign exchange trading, ultimately discover how to trade price action, have great threat- and also finance, and comprehend successful trading psychology.

CHAPTER FIFTEEN

The Psychology of Forex Trading

I have actually been an investor enough time to know a point or regarding just how lots of people think while trading the market. You see, most individuals experience similar thinking patterns as well as emotions as they trade the marketplaces, as well as we can discover numerous crucial points from the distinctions in the method shedding investors think and also the method winning traders assume.

I would be explaining to you the success in the Forex markets, how it depends completely on the system or method you utilize, because it doesn't, it in fact depends mainly on your frame of mind and on just how you think of and respond to the markets.

However, the majority of Forex internet sites attempting to market some indication or robot-based trading system will not inform you this, since they want you to believe that you can make money in the markets simply by buying their trading product. I choose to inform people the truth, as well as the fact is that having an effective and non-confusing trading strategy is extremely important, yet it's only one item of the pie.

The bigger portion of the pie is handling your professions properly as well as handling your emotions correctly, if you do refrain from doing these two points you will never make money in the markets over the lasting.

Why most investors loose cash

You have actually most likely heard that the majority of people that attempt Forex trading end up losing money. There's an excellent reason for this, and also the factor is mainly that many people think of trading in the wrong light. Most individuals come into the markets with unrealistic assumptions, such as assuming they are most likely to stop their jobs after a month of trading or believing they are most likely to turn $1,000 into $100,000 in a few months.

These unrealistic assumptions work to cultivate an account-destroying trading attitude in many investors since they feel way too much stress or "require" to earn money in the markets. When you start patronizing this "requirement" or pressure to earn money, you enviably end up trading emotionally, which is the fastest way to lose your money.

What emotions should you expect in yourself while trading?

To be a little bit extra particular concerning "emotional" trading allows review several of the most usual emotional trading errors that investors make:

Greed

There's an old saying that you might have heard relating to trading the marketplaces, it goes something such as this: "Bulls generate income, bears generate income, as well as pigs obtain butchered". It basically means that if you are a greedy "pig" in the marketplace, you are likely going to shed your cash.

Traders are greedy when they do not take earnings due to the fact that they think a profession is most likely to go for life in their favor. An additional point that greedy traders do is contribute to a placement merely because the marketplace has actually relocated their support, you can include in your trades if you do so for rational cost action-based factors, however doing so just since the market has relocated your support a little, is typically an activity substantiated of greed. Undoubtedly, running the risk of excessive on a trade from the very begin is a greedy thing to do too. The factor right here is that you need to be really careful of greed, since it can creep up on you and swiftly ruin your trading account.

Worry

Traders come to be afraid of getting in the market usually when they are brand-new to trading and have not yet grasped an efficient trading approach like rate action trading (in which situation they ought to not be trading genuine money yet anyways). Worry can also arise in an investor after they hit a collection of losing trades or after enduring a loss larger than what they are psychologically with the ability of soaking up.

To overcome anxiety of the market, you largely have to make certain you are never ever taking the chance of even more money than you are completely okay with losing on a profession. If you are entirely okay with losing the quantity of cash you contend risk, there is nothing to fear. Anxiety can be an extremely limiting feeling to an investor since it can make them lose out on excellent trading chances.

Vengeance

Traders experience a sensation of wanting "revenge" on the market when they suffer a shedding trade that they were "sure" would certainly work out. The crucial thing below is that there is no "certain" thing in trading never.

Additionally, if you have run the risk of way too much money on a profession (beginning to see a motif right here?), as well as you wind up losing that cash, there's a likelihood you are most likely to want to try as well as leap back out there to make that cash back, which normally just leads to one more loss (and occasionally an even bigger one) because you are simply trading psychologically once again.

Euphoria:

While sensation blissful is normally an advantage, it can actually do a great deal of damages to a trader's account after she or he strikes a big winner or a big string of victors. Investors can become overly-confident after winning a couple of trades in the marketplace, consequently most investors experience their largest losing period's right after they hit a number of victors in the market. It is exceptionally alluring to jump right back in the marketplace after a "ideal" trade setup or after you hit 5 winning sell a row, there's a great line between keeping your feet grounded in reality as well as believing that every little thing you do in the marketplaces will certainly turn to gold.

Many traders enter into a tailspin of psychological trading and shedding money after they struck a string of victors. The factor this takes place is because they feel great and also euphoric and ignore the real danger of the marketplace which any trade can lose.

The key to remember here is that trading is a long-term video game of chances, if you have a high-probability trading edge, you will ultimately make money over the long-lasting thinking you follow your trading side with technique. However, even if your edge is 70% successful over time, you can still hit 30 losing sell a row out of 100, so keep this fact in mind as well as always remember you never recognize which trade will be a loser and which will certainly be a winner.

How to get and preserve a reliable trading state of mind

A trader way of thinking is the outcome of doing a lot of points right, as well as it typically takes a mindful effort on the investor's part to accomplish this. It's not always tough to achieve, but if you want to develop an efficient trading mindset, you need to accept specific facts about trading and after that trade the marketplace with these facts in mind.

You need to know what your trading technique (trading edge) is and you require to understand it. You have to become a "sniper" in the market rather than a "device gunner", this includes knowing your trading strategy in and out and also having absolutely no concerns concerning what the marketplace needs to appear like before you risk your hard-earned money in it.

You require to constantly manage your danger correctly. If you do not control your risk on every single trade, you unlock for emotional trading to take hold of your mind, as well as I can promise you that as soon as you start down the domino effect of emotional trading, it can be very hard to stop your slide, and even identify that you are trading emotionally in the first place. You can greatly eliminate the opportunity of ending up being an overly-emotional investor by just running the risk of an amount of cash per trade that you are 100% alright with losing. You must expect to lose on any offered trade, this way, you are constantly familiar with the actual opportunity of it in fact taking place.

You require not to over-trade. A lot of investors trade way too much. You need to recognize what your trading side is with 100% certainty and then only trade when it's present. When you start trading even if you "seem like it" or since you "type of" see your trading side, you start a roller rollercoaster of psychological trading that can be extremely tough to quit. Do not start over trading and you will likely not end up being an emotional Forex trader.

You require to end up being an arranged investor. If there is something that is the "adhesive" that holds every one of the factors You need to think about Forex trading like an organization rather than like a trip to the online casino. Be calm as well as determining in all your interactions with the marketplace and you need to have no worry maintaining the emotional trading satanic forces at bay.

Technique

You require to recognize that no amount of goals setting without discipline can result in success. You cannot do well in trading without discipline. Nobody can succeed in any organization, let alone trading without outright discipline.

Self-control is the bedrock of successful investors. It's the discipline that different human success from human failing, effective investors from not successful investors, winning professions from losing trades. It allows you to remain adhesive with your goal and need. I cannot be remarkably delighted without discipline, similarly we cannot be remarkably arranged, wealthy, as well as intelligent with no type of self-control.

In my view and from interactions with few traders, trading system is ranked far below self-control as well as finance in the ladder of success in the trading business. The very best location to satisfy people of excellent up-and-comers, investors, traders, authors, etc. is the club of technique. It's the only criterion that divides you from million traders.

A technique individual recognizes he must want to devote 100% of his time as well as various other sources to the success of a picked career. Whatever it takes, he's prepared to endure. The capability to perform each profession as planned is discipline. When you follow up your trading system as well as plans, you work out excellent discipline.

The trading system might be well back-tested and trusted, its discipline that will certainly makes it work and also efficient. No system can be 100% precise and also create 100% winning trades in all time thus during the drawdown, its self-control that will make you take the loser rapidly and transfer to next trade, adhere to the system as long as you count on workability and dependability that in the future it will produce profits. The discipline of the trader shows up in his decision taking. When you are trading, always advise yourself that technique in terms of acceptance of the outcome of the cause whichever means is taking responsibility.

You have to accept the risk prior to you open any kind of position. Trading ought to be treated like a business, uplifting on your own from realm of subconscious state of psychological and sensible incompetence to mental and also emotional state of competence is as result of appropriate preparation and also technique.

When you get into a tight place as well as every little thing breaks you, till it seems as though you cannot hold on a min much longer, never ever give up after that for that is simply the area as well as time that the trend will transform says Harriet Beecher Stowe. My experience has truly aided to make simple classification of discipline in trading. Emotional, System and also Professional Discipline A trader may not be excellent in all however must aim to boost each day.

Psychological Discipline.

I have actually checked out publications upon books about exactly how to get rid of feeling from trading yet I have not seen any individual that has actually effectively eliminated feeling from trading. I have actually only seen individuals who recognize their emotion. You can not entirely remove emotion from trading - never. But considering that you recognize now that your self-awareness is one of the most essential technique variables, you can use any type of degree of your emotion to your benefit (aware and also unconscious).

There is sensible difference between being aware of feelings as well as acting to transform. The feeling writers as well as other traders are trying to describe is the subconscious feeling. These 2 feelings require not be generalized as feeling cannot be completely eradicated in trading. The way to function it out is through technique and understanding by bringing the unpredictable subconscious emotion to security. The minute emotion enters awareness, analysis embed in.

From emotional viewpoint it's recognized that unconscious activity is brought right into recognition, it registers in the cortex as well as the cortex can assess things anew, make a decision to change the outlook. Feeling belongs to decision making, analyzing it makes it logical.

Traders usually are tricked by price actions of the marketplace by the pressure of customers as well as vendors that try hard to press the rate activity to their desirable placement. The rate may not be true worth of a specific underlying tool yet the force of feelings by purchasers and sellers at that specific time triggered it.

Given that trading the markets are zero-sum deals it is not mathematically feasible to ever understand with certainty that any type of profession presumption or thinking will certainly be right except later on after the setting has been opened. Nevertheless, as cost discount rates the true state of the market at any kind of specific time, a trader needs to recognize that the cost exists because that's where it should be and also, it's caused by the force of need and supply. So, if you as a trader really feel indifference concerning the existing cost, the capability to stay in serenity and also calmness setting despite the cost activity movement without pressure of emotion to take unjustified professions is what I refer as Emotional Discipline.

You should at some time on the market 'Stand down'. Not do anything aside from enjoying the force of other purchasers and vendors out there. When you are psychologically disciplined you will certainly stay with the concept of stillness, peace as well as stay clear of turmoil brought on by various other traders especially when you cannot absorb aspect of understanding in dominating market instructions. Remember we fear what we do not comprehend.

Specialist Self-control

No one knows all. Nobody has all the answers. Knowing that you do not know anything is far better than assuming that you know a lot when you truly don't. An expert trader understands what he doesn't know, his weak point as well as offset it. This capability of an investor to know what he does not understand and technique himself to look for knowledge as well as education for improvement in order to be a far better trader not minding the expense is what I called Specialist Technique. It's a well-known truth that just 3% of viewers check out an entire publication starting from phase one. Very same most likely to what is being found out or taught. The only 3% investors who strive for enhancement day-to-day get to the specialist degree. To reach expert degree education and learning is the vital and also the only way. Nothing takes place till it is self-control.

Indiscipline vision is a babble vision, indiscipline traders are failed investors.

Expert self-control starts with your mind. You have to unclutter your mind from prejudices effect of the marketplace. Direct your focus and also mindset on the important point that is taking place not what you assume must happen in the market. Aim to be a better investor, work on yourself and also perspective.

System Discipline

The typical saying by investors and also analysts is Strategy your trade as well as trade your strategy, yet only couple of investors adhere to this straightforward regulation. The premise of system discipline is your capability to discipline on your own to trade your system, accept the danger and also end result of your professions, win or loss after you have examined the system.

The very best trading system often seems idiotically simple to some traders who are unfamiliar with this type of trading. It's the system self-control that embraces your edge after taking into consideration offered mathematical realities and also variables and also emotional detachment from the market. Maybe in the world of trading, no matter just how discipline you are, you will experience losers.

Your system will certainly fail to produce profit. This is not new; all trading system has drawdown time. Approve and also improve it. Bear in mind stopping working or shedding profession is a step better to a winning profession. Be strategically technique as well as understand when things are not functioning, therefore quit. I am not much better in this regards or victim of any one of the discipline like other behavioral patterns of market individuals. Be a sensible trader who picks up from blunders of others.

CONCLUSION

This brings me to the end of this book on Trading. Thank you again for buying this book! I wish it has aided you get an excellent, understanding of just how the whole trading market is operate, purposely maintained the explanations basic and uncomplicated so everyone can comprehend it.

You do not require to be bamboozled with technological and complex lingo. Much like driving an auto where you don't require to know how everything jobs, as long as you understand, how to drive it and also recognize the roadway rules. The very same apply on Foreign Exchange Trading. Some people attempt to make it appear more difficult than it is, but having stated that, it is not as straightforward as it looks to be a consistently profitable trader. There are a lot of aspects to be taken into consideration, yet like anything, if you practice enough as well as learn by your errors, you can go on to be a part of the platform.

A change state of mind can be tough for aiming investors to take on yet is crucial to be successful in the foreign exchange market. The most important thing is to stay clear of looking for confirmation, which doesn't exist in the market, and believe in chances.

CPSIA information can be obtained
at www.ICGtesting.com
Printed in the USA
LVHW082239250422
717205LV00026B/708